Robin Kermode is one of Europe's leading communication coaches; working with senior executives, entrepreneurs, politicians, charities, corporate teams, professionals and media personalities.

As an actor, he is a well-known face to audiences on television and the London stage. He is a popular voice-over artist, presenter and keynote speaker at conferences.

As a professional writer, Robin advises clients on the structure and content of their message. His input into pitch preparation has helped many companies win new business.

Robin was born in Lancashire, the son of a headmaster. He is married and lives in London.

www.robinkermode.com

One of the best speakers I have ever heard.
Tracey Morgan - Senior HR Manager, Bank of America

Personalised, focused and remarkably effective.
Juliet Wedderburn - MD, PWM DeutscheBank London

Robin has wit, charm and professionalism.
Francois Curiel - Chairman, Christie's, Europe

Robin has a great ability to build empathy very quickly.
Nigel Sullivan - Group HRD, Talk Talk plc

The best talk I've ever seen at the LHRC.
John Maxted - Chair, London HR Connection

If you want someone to drive an impact into your business ...
call Robin.
Rupert Keane - CEO, Emap Insight

Robin has a rare ability to talk to everybody individually - even
in a larger group.
David James - Senior Manager, L&D UK, The Walt Disney Company

Robin's training was delivered with humour and personality with
a long lasting impact.
Pierre Lever - CEO, Planet Retail

I recommend Robin to anyone who wants to up their game in
communications.
Martyn Dawes - Founder, Coffee Nation

Practical insights, tools, personal energy and humour ... for even
the most nervous of aspiring presenters.
Mike Hind - Communications Manager, CAP

Robin has given my team confidence, building on their
individual styles with surprisingly rapid results.
Rob Keve - CEO, Fizzback

Delightfully simple and readable - a memorable pocket coach.
Davia CM Carter - The Mentor - author of BREAKTHROUGH

I can't remember when I last learned so much that was so useful
in so little time.
Andy Atkins - Executive Director, Friends of the Earth

SPEAK

SO YOUR AUDIENCE
WILL LISTEN

7 steps to confident and successful public speaking

ROBIN KERMODE

Copyright © Robin Kermode 2013

First published in Great Britain in 2013
by Pendle Publishing

The right of Robin Kermode to be identified as the author of
this work has been asserted by him in accordance with the
Copyright, Designs and Patents Act 1988.

A CIP record for this title is available from the
British Library

ISBN 978-0955530111

Pendle Publishing
www.pendlepublishing.co.uk

With thanks to my clients
who have taught me so much.

Welcome

Resources

Welcome

In my early twenties, I was asked to give a Best Man speech at a friend's wedding. I was petrified.

I couldn't understand why I felt so bad since I was an actor and was used to standing up in front of an audience. But I realised that as the Best Man I would be standing up there as myself saying my own words, not as a character in a play saying the playwright's words. If it all went wrong it would be my head on the block and I hated the whole experience.

So I started to look at why we feel so emotionally exposed when we give a speech.

Most of us are quite relaxed and confident when we're with our friends and family. We can tell a story or even tell a joke. But put us on a platform, and ask us to tell a story or tell a joke, and we can feel very different.

When we speak to an audience, we often put on a public mask and use a different voice. Why can't we seem to be ourselves when we give a talk?

Why can we seem to connect with an audience one day, and not another?

How should we best structure a talk and prepare our notes? And how can we deal with nerves?

In this book we will look at all aspects of spoken communication, from structure right through to delivery.

We will learn how we can tread that fine line between confidence and arrogance and start to drop that public mask. We will learn how we can be physically dynamic, yet still open and relaxed.

We will learn how to have a conversation with our audience so that we connect with them every time we speak and deliver our message with energy, clarity and humanity.

Ideally, what we want is a really strong message delivered in a very conversational way. What we don't want is a strong message delivered too strongly - or we'll come across as over-slick and possibly over-coached. And we can't have a soft message delivered too softly - or it will all fall apart like blancmange.

If all this sounds a bit daunting, don't worry. In 7 simple steps you can learn to be a confident and successful speaker. There are specific exercises at the end of every section for you to practice.

Reading this book could change the way you speak to everyone in both your business and your personal life. It is a book for anyone who has to deliver a message, tell a story or speak to another human being.

So whether you're a CEO presenting to shareholders, a manager motivating your team, an entrepreneur pitching for new business, a head teacher talking to pupils, a charity worker asking for donations or a parent speaking at your daughter's wedding, this book will help you to become a confident and successful speaker.

And, hopefully, you'll enjoy the experience too.

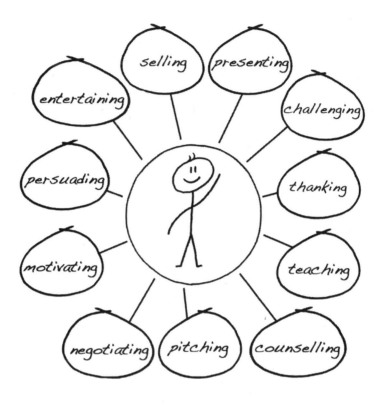

1

Your Confidence

The two most common questions I am asked on a daily basis are, 'How can I be more confident?' and 'How can I be more charismatic?'

Who is the most confident and charismatic person you can think of?

Chances are you've thought of a well-known person from the world of politics, business or the arts. If we met someone like that at a drinks party, I'm pretty sure we'd think they were charismatic. But we often project confidence and charisma onto famous people when we meet them.

Some people are born performers. I can think of several people who don't need a spotlight at all; they start performing the moment the fridge door light comes on.

Are these people really confident on the inside?

I think we've all seen enough showbiz documentaries to know that many performers suffer from lack of self-esteem, even depression, sometimes using their dramatic or comedic skills as a shield.

As a child my hero was the actor Richard Burton but I know if I'd actually met him I would probably have been a gibbering wreck, totally unable to speak to him. I would have been in no state to judge how charismatic he really was.

So think of the most confident, charismatic person you know personally. Choose someone who is not a public figure. Some of the most impressive people I've met have not been famous - but when they walk into a room the energy seems to change.

What have these confident, charismatic people got in common and what are they doing that makes them change the energy of a room?

Dropping the public mask

People often say they feel exposed when they stand up to present or to give a talk. They say this even in a family situation. Being asked to say a few impromptu words at a family party can be frightening for many, so it's not always the pressure of a hostile audience that causes problems - even in the bosom of our loving family we can feel nervous.

Being the centre of attention can make us feel exposed. What is it that we're so frightened of? Not being clever enough? Not being interesting enough? Not looking foolish? Failing miserably?

One thing we do know is that we are all human, and that our audience is also human. It is human to have imperfections and insecurities. In fact, many of our favourite entertainers show us their vulnerability and it is often for that very reason that we love them more. We can identify with them. It's very hard to identify with someone who appears to have no insecurity, no human vulnerability at all.

Standing on a podium just being ourselves, not hiding behind our public face, showing the real person inside us with all our natural human insecurities, is an idea that many of us find daunting.

To some extent we all, at times, wear our public mask. But it would be great if we could start to drop the public mask when giving a speech and allow our true selves to shine. And I promise you, this is not as frightening as it might seem.

Confidence and charisma

To understand how we can become more confident and charismatic, we first have to understand what confidence and charisma are in the first place.

We all think we know what they look like from the outside. We could describe the way a person moves, the way they sound, their energy and their enthusiasm. We might say they have a certain 'something', an 'X factor' or an 'aura'. They appear to light up a room when they enter. But it's often easier to see these qualities in someone else than to feel them in ourselves.

The modern world seems to place a high value on confidence, particularly social confidence - often valuing it more highly than confidence in other areas. So someone might be skilled and confident in one area of their life - for example, brain surgery - but not necessarily confident in a social situation. We might assume that a brain surgeon would be socially confident but I don't think there is necessarily any correlation between being skilled at something and feeling socially confident. Hopefully, a brain surgeon wouldn't lack medical confidence during an operation but it is perfectly possible for them to lack social confidence when not in the operating theatre.

If we took a survey of everyone on the planet and asked them on a scale of 1 to 10 if they felt confident, I suspect the results would be pretty low. Many of us have learnt to appear confident, particularly in the workplace. We have learnt to put on a public mask of confidence, but we all know that is not the same as feeling truly confident inside.

Most sociologists agree that up to about the age of four or five years old we are looking outwards, learning about the world each moment and finding it fascinating. After that we begin to look inwards, becoming more aware of our role and our place in the scheme of things. We are more concerned about fitting in and not looking foolish. We don't want to appear weak or stupid, so damage limitation slowly and insidiously creeps in. Everything we do is designed to save us from failing or looking ridiculous, but sadly that often results in the very thing we're trying to prevent.

Confident people seem to have avoided this trap. They are constantly looking outwards, learning about the world and still finding it fascinating. They appear to be unconcerned about what the world thinks of them. They seem happy with who they are. They don't appear to need to hide behind a public mask. It's an enviable position to be in.

Now what about charisma - that X factor we spoke of earlier? Some people can hold an audience in the palm of their hand without appearing to have a single nerve in their body.

These people don't seem to need approval. They seem so self-assured that they don't appear to be concerned about what we think of them. They appear to be more interested in us than in themselves.

Charisma is an extension of confidence and is about humanity and connection. It is about making other people feel special.

At this point you might say to me, 'That's OK for other people but I'm not in that enviable position. I don't feel particularly charismatic or confident. I can recognise those qualities in other people but I don't think I will ever have them myself.'

Don't worry. There is good news here. There are tools that can help us appear more confident - and the more we appear to be confident, the more we will gradually begin to feel confident. I promise you, it is possible for all of us to become more confident and charismatic. In fact, it's really quite easy.

In the 21st century, we want speakers to be relaxed, natural and honest. We don't want 'pushy'. We don't want to be sold to - whether it's a product or an idea. We have become 'advertising aware'. We know when we are being sold to and we know when someone isn't being honest. What we crave is authenticity.

So what is authenticity? What does it look like? How do we become more authentic when we speak? And how can we reach out and connect authentically with our audience?

Most of us feel that we are able to be ourselves - be authentic - when we are relaxing with friends and family, but often nerves and the pressure of certain situations pull us 'off centre'. The voice that comes out of our mouths isn't our normal voice and our bodies start to behave in weird ways. Even our choice of words can seem unnatural.

But the good news is that if we are able to be ourselves in our private life, then we can learn to be ourselves in our public life.

In this book we'll learn, in simple steps, how to stay relaxed and be 'ourselves' even in difficult situations; how to be more effective and truly connect with our audience at a deep level.

We'll look at how best to structure a talk or presentation, how to prepare our notes and learn how we can deliver our message with energy, clarity and humanity.

And as we learn to become more authentic, we'll gradually begin to feel more confident and become more charismatic.

Let's start at the beginning ...

Become who you are

I saw a poster in a café a few years ago with this phrase, *BECOME WHO YOU ARE*. I loved it. I think it means we should try to re-connect with the person we really are, as opposed to the public persona that we have become and now show to the world.

In our teenage years we often spent hours trying to fit in, trying to be like everyone else. It is no wonder then that as an adult, we have to remind ourselves constantly to become who we really are. Or rather, who we were - until we started trying to fit in.

So let's try to become ourselves.

I want you to be the best possible version of yourself that you can be when speaking in public. And remember, there isn't just one way of public speaking. There are some basic ideas, of course, that can help us keep on track but also many different styles of delivering a speech.

Clients often say to me that they want to have the charisma and gravitas of a world leader. But there are two dangers here.

Firstly, we shouldn't try to be like someone else. If we do, we end up 'acting' and unless we are trained actors, acting rarely works. It will usually come across as false. And if you're presenting to people you know, they'll soon spot that this is not the real you.

Secondly, we generally see world leaders speaking to millions of people on the world stage. This is a very different style of public speaking. It requires a higher level of gravitas, and probably a slower pace, than would normally be appropriate in the settings in which we usually operate.

Imagine Barack Obama at breakfast, pouring milk on his cereal, making a ridiculously grand speech at the breakfast table to his wife, Michelle …

'And I say this to you, Michelle, our milk will flow. And it will flow freely. But our milk will not flow if it is not poured. And so I will take it upon my own person to pour this milk, Michelle. And remember, this is not just any milk - it is the milk of human kindness. As I pour this milk today, Michelle, let us start our day's journey together, united in a shared cereal, a shared coffee, a shared breakfast.'

You get the idea. Epic speeches might be appropriate, and might work, on the world stage but not in a board meeting and certainly not at the breakfast table.

So let's not try to be like anyone else. Let's become who we are.

Make-up guru, Bobby Brown, says that make-up should make you look like you - only prettier.

And so when we speak in public, we should still look and sound like us - only us in the best possible light.

Audiences will warm to us if we show our human side. We don't want to be slick and we don't have to be perfect.

Perfect is weird.

Pina Bousccht, the dancer and choreographer, said that audiences love her dancers even more at the end of a show, 'because they have given something of themselves'. At a deep level they have shown us their humanity. They weren't aiming for perfection, they were aiming for authenticity and humanity.

I see people in business life every day who think that in a business environment being professional is more appropriate and effective than being human. But being emotionally open and showing our human side will always work if we trust it. In fact, so few people show their genuine humanity when speaking in public that we are truly blown away when we come across someone who does.

There's a great Russian proverb: 'When you meet a man you judge him by his clothes, but when you leave him you judge him by his heart.' And the same is true of speeches and presentations. We so often try to be what we think other people want us to be - but remember Shakespeare: 'To thine own self be true.'

I often think that adults have forgotten to how to play. We may play sport but often only competitively. We're usually more concerned about not losing than enjoying it.

But children seem to be able to play just for the sake of it. There is a wonderful freedom in that. In his poem *The Human Child*, W.B. Yeats sums it up brilliantly:

'To and fro we leap
And chase the frothy bubbles,
While the world is full of troubles
And anxious in its sleep.'

So the next time we give a talk, let us play, have fun and chase those frothy bubbles.

My younger brother and sister played tennis as juniors and the house was always full of silver cups that they'd won. Hundreds of them. Well, perhaps not hundreds but that's what it felt like to me. One day, the parents of another tennis player said to me, 'Don't you feel really unsuccessful with all these cups on show? Where are the cups that you've won?'

I hadn't won any, of course, but despite appearing in a TV sitcom at the time, the comment irked me.

So I decided then and there to buy myself a cup. It was a little silver cup about 5 cm high on a tiny black plinth. I had it inscribed, *'The Robin Cup. For Being Robin'.*

And it sits on my mantlepiece to this day.

I think we should all buy ourselves a cup and have it inscribed. It would be a constant reminder to us that being ourselves is enough.

It is not only enough, it is better.

What does confidence look like?

Let's imagine you and I are sitting together at a roadside café and we're watching people walking up and down on the pavement in front of us. We're going to decide purely by watching them, who looks confident and who does not. We know nothing about them, we haven't heard them speak, but we're going to mark them down on our chart. A tick for confident. A cross for not confident. We'll be judging harshly today.

After all, that's what we do when we sit in an audience watching a speaker take the stage. Before they've even started speaking we've made all sorts of instant judgements about them. Are they going to be interesting, funny, boring or rubbish? We're often a hard crowd to please.

Malcolm Gladwell, in his brilliant book *Blink*, suggests that we make these decisions in the blink of an eye. We don't really even have a minute to win over our audience. It's like that line from the film *Jerry Maguire*, 'You had me at Hello'. That's what we should be aiming for.

So there we are sitting with our pieces of paper at our roadside café, noting down our ticks and crosses as people walk up and down in front of us. Confident. Not confident. Confident. Not confident.

On what are we basing our judgements? We know nothing about these people but we continue to make our snap judgements anyway. Most people will say that it has something to do with their body language and how they hold themselves. That's true, of course, but surely it's more subtle than saying that someone who walks tall with a sense of purpose is confident, and someone who walks slowly with their head down is not confident.

We watch a man in a light blue suit walk by, his chest forward, smiling broadly with his head held high. Would we put a tick for confident or a cross for not confident?

Next there is a man in an overcoat, walking very slowly looking at the ground. Do we give him a tick or a cross?

And now a lady in a green dress carrying a newspaper. She smiles and stops to check her watch. A tick or a cross?

How did these unsuspecting members of the public fare on our score sheets?

Let's start with the man in the light blue suit. Initially we might have ticked 'confident', as he was walking with a positive energy, chest out, his head held high. But there's a fine line between confidence and arrogance. A very fine line. Our judgement of him would depend on which side of that line he was. If he had veered into arrogance we might have marked him down as 'not confident'.

Confident people don't have to try to make an impression. Arrogant people often do. And sometimes people who try too hard to make an impression, over-compensating for their insecurity, can come across as under-confident.

What about the man in the overcoat? Initially, we might have marked him down as 'not confident' because he was walking with his head down. But what if he had been on his way to an important meeting and was thinking about what he was going to say there?

And the lady in the green dress? She was smiling, so we might think 'confident'. But then she stopped to check her watch.

Body language is a very subtle business. We have to try to guess why she was stopping to check her watch and why she was smiling. Was she checking her watch because was afraid of being late or to see if she had time for a leisurely coffee? Was she smiling because she was genuinely happy or was she smiling because she was feeling sad, and had 'painted' on a smile to appear happier than she actually was?

There are hundreds of signals that we will all pick up in the blink of an eye.

If after half an hour of watching these people, we compared our notes of the hundreds we had seen, I suspect our 'confident' and 'not confident' columns would probably match up. We would have both made our individual snap judgements, our *blinks*, but despite knowing nothing about these people, we would have both agreed on who we felt looked confident and who we felt didn't.

Why would our *blinks* have been so similar?

Well, there is one thing that all the people in our 'confident' list have in common. And one thing that all the people in our 'not confident' list do not have.

It's a physical thing. Something in their bodies. Any idea what it is?

The bottom line is that all the people we had ticked as looking 'confident' will have had a low centre of gravity.

And where is their centre of gravity?

It is in their lower stomach. Below their belly button.

Their gut.

Let me explain:

Low Centre of Gravity

If you've ever done yoga, pilates or any martial arts, you'll have heard of what they call the 'core' or the 'centre'. Anything we do from our core has more power.

The police are taught to work out where a person's centre of gravity is. If someone with a high centre of gravity is being threatening towards them, then it's not too worrying. But someone with a low centre of gravity could be a serious threat.

Imagine I was walking down the street and a man rushed up to me and shouted, 'Give me your wallet'. In my head I'd probably be thinking, 'No, I'm sorry but I don't think I will' - unless he had a low centre of gravity, in which case I'd definitely take him more seriously.

So having a low centre of gravity can make us appear confident and powerful.

At this point, I would like to stress that I'm not trying to encourage you to come across as a psychopath when giving a talk or presentation, but I would like you to come across as confident and believable.

I would like you to have a low centre of gravity so that when you next walk on stage to give a talk, the entire audience will give you an instant tick for 'confident'. But they will only do that if you have a low centre of gravity.

EXERCISE 1

Stand facing a wall and focus on picture or a light switch.

Imagine you are going to give a talk. Start by saying:

'Good morning, Ladies and Gentlemen, my name is ..., I have some exciting news for you.'

Say it directly to the picture or the light switch.

Now say it again, but before you say it, tighten your buttocks or your thighs. Really clench them tight. Stick with me on this one - it does work.

Now say the sentence again, but this time without tightening your buttocks or your thighs.

And once again with them tightened.

Do this a few times, with and without clenching.

Do you feel any different either way?

Most people say that with their buttocks or their thighs clenched and tight, they feel stronger and more 'centred'.

What is happening is that by clenching those big muscles, you are lowering your centre of gravity. And if you lower your centre of gravity, you will both feel and appear more centred and confident.

EXERCISE 2

Over the next 24 hours, try to keep your centre of gravity low by clenching your buttocks or your thighs when standing still.

You can try this in almost any social situation. Standing in the supermarket queue, at a drinks party or at work. No one will be aware that you are clenching away. Unless you are wearing shorts or a short skirt, most clothes will completely mask your actions.

Observe how you feel when you are doing this.

Do you behave differently?

Do other people treat you differently?

If you can keep your centre of gravity low, you will not only appear more confident, you will begin to feel more confident.

EXERCISE 3

Obviously you can't clench your buttocks or your thighs as you're walking - you would look very odd. Instead try to become aware where your centre of gravity is as you walk about.

First, try walking as if your centre of gravity is in your upper chest? Imagine you are being pulled along by a piece of string attached to your upper chest.

How do you feel when you do this? Do you feel 'lighter' or 'heavier'? Do you walk at a different speed? Do you feel more or less confident? Just observe.

Now try walking as if your centre of gravity is in your lower stomach. Imagine you are being pulled along by a piece of rope attached to your lower stomach.

How do you feel when you do this? Do you feel 'lighter' or 'heavier'? Do you walk at a different speed?

Do you feel more or less centred than when your centre of gravity is in your upper chest?

Do you feel more confident when your centre of gravity is in your lower stomach than when it is in your upper chest?

At this stage just observe how you feel.

2

Your Connection

'Only connect! That was the whole of her sermon. Only connect the prose and the passion, and both will be exalted, and human love will be seen at its height.' (E.M.Forster, *Howards End*)

When we meet someone, when we speak in a meeting or when we stand on stage, we have less than ten seconds to connect with our audience. We have less than ten seconds to to 'win them over'. The way we move, speak and stand will all affect the way we are judged.

We have already established that when we first meet someone or see them giving a speech, we make pretty quick judgements about them. The automatic part of our brain will make rapid associations mostly based on past experience. Almost in an instant, we think we have a sense of who this person is. Are they going to be interesting, funny or boring? Do they look professional, confident and experienced? We can judge harshly when it's not us standing up there.

But if we make instant judgements of other people, then we can be sure that they will be making instant judgements of us. So we'd better make sure we do everything we can to help them judge us in the way we want them to. We must learn to give off the best signals, right from the start.

So how do we make sure that we connect with every audience every time? And in under ten seconds?

The Three Zones of Communication

We all have three zones of communication. Imagine a circular zone around your body - an area where you feel happy in your own personal space, your own personal world.

Of course, the size of circle will depend on the space around you but essentially this circular zone is your metaphorical personal space.

This is your Zone One.

Everyone has their own Zone One - including, of course, each and every member of your audience.

Next we have our Zone Two. This is a wider circular metaphorical zone around us. Again the size will depend on the space we are in. In the boardroom, our Zone Two might be a couple of meters wide or the length of the table; in a large hall speaking to 500 people, it would be even wider.

And again, remember every member of the audience also has their own Zone Two.

Zone Two is a space that is open and welcoming. It is an area where we have metaphorically reached out to other people.

And lastly, we have our Zone Three.

This is an even wider metaphorical circle than Zone Two. It is wider because it's about pushing outwards. It's about taking control, often with a loud volume. It ultimately feels aggressive and confrontational.

We can't see these three Zones, of course. They are metaphorical, as I say, but they are there. And if we can become aware of them, we can learn to truly connect with our audience.

Let me explain.

A customer walks into my shop. I could choose to ignore her and stay in my own personal space, my Zone One.

ME   CUSTOMER

But I naturally want to make her feel welcome, so I metaphorically and emotionally move into my Zone Two.

I might smile and say, 'Can I help you?' or 'Are you looking for anything in particular?' I haven't necessarily moved physically at all but I have made a mental move into the wider emotional space that we call Zone Two. Zone Two is where we are 'open' and 'welcoming'.

ME   CUSTOMER

Now if I am being open and welcoming, in my Zone Two, and my customer stays 'closed' in her Zone One, my communication with her is still blocked.

So I now have two choices. I could retreat back into my Zone One and say to myself, 'Well, I offered help, but she wasn't interested.' In this case my communication with her would have failed.

Or I could advance further, pushing harder and becoming louder, 'Come on, don't be shy.' This is unlikely to encourage her to move into her Zone Two. She is far more likely to retreat deeper into the safety of her Zone One.

By advancing further, pushing harder and becoming louder, I would have moved into my Zone Three.

And where is my Zone Three?

Correct - her Zone One. Effectively I would have invaded her emotional space. And none of us like that.

Zone Three is generally loud, controlling and pompous. It is self-congratulatory and ultimately 'un-welcoming'.

Clearly any communication that starts from Zone Three will not work well.

Here's the thing - the only way we can communicate is if both parties are in their Zone Two.

So if I am open, relaxed and welcoming in my Zone Two, and I can encourage my customer to join me in her Zone Two, then we stand a good chance of our communication going well. Where my Zone Two and her Zone Two overlap, we can truly connect.

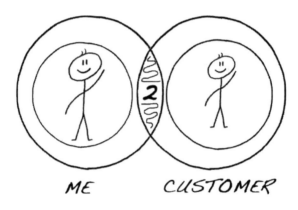

ME   CUSTOMER

So when we stand up to give a talk, we have to actively choose to reach out and metaphorically go into our Zone Two if we are to stand any chance of connecting with our audience. And, of course, it will only work well if we can encourage our audience to join us in their Zone Two.

But if we go into our Zone Three and become too loud, controlling or arrogant, we effectively lock our audience into their Zone Ones. When this happens, communication is blocked and is unlikely to go well.

So all communication should ideally take place in Zone Two.

This is all very well and good, you might say, 'But where is my Zone Two? I can't see it. I can't feel it. I don't even know which Zone I'm in - let alone how to switch my Zone to suit the situation.'

That's ok. Just let the concept sit for a little while. It will all become clear.

Think of the kind of people you like to spend time with. The kind of people who make you feel welcome. Do they shout at you? Or do they chat with you? Does a conversation with them feel like a conversation or more like a one-sided lecture?

The next time you meet someone, or you have to give a talk, just ask yourself, 'Was I open and welcoming? Was I in my Zone Two? Was I encouraging them to join me in their Zone Two? Or was I being quiet and retiring in my Zone One? Or being loud, pushy and cocky in my Zone Three?' If you are being honest with yourself, you'll know which Zone you were in. It's pretty easy to work it out once you start to think about it.

The traits of the Zones can be subtle but here's a very simple snapshot of what the Zones look like:

A person in Zone One is not interested in reaching out to talk to another person. They are happy to be on their own, in their own personal space. Their energy is generally low.

A person in Zone Two is happy to reach out to talk. Their energy is both relaxed and dynamic.

A person in Zone Three is not interested in listening to someone else. They will be domineering and loud. Their energy is generally high and controlling.

So how do we feel when we meet someone who is in their Zone Two?

They make us feel welcome and that they have time for us. They appear to be listening to us and seem to understand how we might be feeling.

If we were in an audience listening to a speaker who was in their Zone Two, we would feel that they were concerned about us rather than simply being concerned about themselves.

So if we want to speak so our audience will listen, we must learn to be in our Zone Two when we are speaking. We must always be in Zone Two if we want our communication to be effective, powerful and fun.

We have all sat in an audience where the speaker talks *at* us. I'm sure it happened at school and I know it happens at work. Talking *at* us or *down* to us is a common mistake, and is clearly the behaviour of someone in Zone Three.

I often work with clients on executive boards who travel around speakinng to the wider company. The top brass are sent out to spread the company message and check out the mood in the regions.

Now, imagine you're attending a regional talk being given by a member of the executive board who's come down from head office to see how things are going in your neck of the woods. How might you be feeling before you go into the hall?

If you're wearing your cynical hat, you might be worried that there will be announcements of redundancies, wage freezes or relocations. You may think you'll be told off for not delivering on schedule or not implementing a new company policy. And, as usual, at the Question and Answer session afterwards the speaker will pretend to listen to your concerns but take no real notice of you at all. At best it will be boring. At worst you'll be for the high jump.

That might well be your mind-set as you enter the hall. And possibly the mind-set of the rest of the audience as you sit waiting.

Meanwhile the 'Fat Cat' from head office is being driven down the motorway in his limousine, classical music gently playing on the audio system as he chats on the mobile to his PA. (You get the picture.) His mind-set might be in a very different space to that of the waiting members of the audience. And unless he is able to move himself into his Zone Two and encourage his audience to move into their individual Zone Twos, then this meeting will be a complete waste of time.

If he starts off in Zone Three - loud, over confident and controlling - he'll confirm all our cynical suspicions and he'll never win us round and we probably won't listen to a word he says.

We want to encourage our audience to move into their Zone Two, so that they hear our message with energy, clarity and humanity.

To do that we must be in our Zone 2 from the start.

Then we must encourage our audience to join us in their Zone 2.

How can we make sure we do that?

Here are ten key points that will encourage each and every member of the audience to join us in their Zone Two:

1. It's not about you

We've all been at parties or networking events where we have met someone who is the very opposite of this. Someone who says, 'IT'S ALL ABOUT ME'. These are the kind of people we might call 'boring'. They're boring because they don't listen. They're not really interested in us and they will tell the same stories about how great they are to anyone who will stay long enough to be bored by them.

We want to feel valued. All human beings do. So when we meet someone new, we should always try to make them feel special. Remember, it's about them. It's not about you. In fact, it's never about you.

There's an old actors' joke: an actor has been holding forth at a drinks party about his latest film for too long and eventually says, 'Well that's enough about me. What do *you* think about me.' A prime example of Zone Three behaviour. No listening, no empathy and it's clearly ALL ABOUT HIM.

Henry Ford said, 'A business absolutely devoted to service will only have one worry about profits. They will be embarrassingly large.' And a speaker absolutely devoted to engaging their audience will only have one worry about their applause. It will be embarrassingly loud and embarrassingly long.

So if we can remember to be in our Zone Two, our audience will feel welcomed and valued. We must make them feel that we are interested in them and in what they might think and feel. Hopefully they will then want to join us in their individual Zone Twos and will want to listen to our message. How great will that be?

2. Empathy

Let's go back to the regional talk scenario we looked at just now. If the executive from head office is in his Zone Two right from the start and encourages his audience to join him there, he stands a good chance of them wanting to listen to him. He could speed up this process up by acknowledging where his audience's mind-set might be.

For example, if he senses that they are already bored, he might say, 'This meeting is going to be different. I'm not going to bore you for hours. I'm going to speak for exactly seven minutes and then I'd like to know what you think.'

If there had been rumours of redundancies, he might start with, 'Rumours have been flying around like wildfire. Many of them are, in fact, incorrect. I'd like to tell you clearly what our plans really are.'

What we can never do is ignore 'the elephant in the room'.

If he spoke for an hour before getting to the part the audience is concerned about, then they wouldn't have listened to one word that he'd said up to then. He would have wasted an hour of his time and theirs. So let's always address 'the elephant in the room' - or at least refer to it early on.

It's never easy to give bad news to an audience. Sometimes we try to avoid it. Sometimes we skirt around the problem desperately trying to avoid the embarrassment of saying it. And sometimes we even lie.

But there's a golden rule - if it has to be said, let's say it cleanly, with empathy.

If we want to encourage our audience to join us in their individual Zone Twos, then we must have empathy with them. We must always try to put ourselves in their shoes.

3. Equal Status

People will only connect with us if we give them respect and we respect ourselves.

We must give each other equal status.

But pressured situations, like a job interview or giving an important talk, often make us either give too much power to the audience or, as a compensation for nerves, too much power to ourselves.

If we're in the audience and we see a speaker who looks like they are intimidated by us, we can very easily lose respect for them. And we'll probably discredit their argument as well.

Getting our audience into their Zone Two is about making them feel special, whilst still respecting ourselves.

Of course, over-confidence is just as bad as under-confidence.

Sometimes nerves attack and we try to cover this up. We try to appear confident and full of self-esteem but this can make us seem pushy and arrogant. Nothing could be further from the truth when we're a gibbering wreck inside. But if the audience thinks that we're a bit cocky and full of self-importance, they will read it as Zone Three behaviour. And as we know, Zone Three behaviour will not make them either like us or want to join us in their Zone Two.

We like to meet confident people but we never want them to cross into arrogance. Truly confident people make us feel important. They are confident enough in themselves to know that they don't have to make it all about them. We want them to make us feel special.

We must avoid coming across as arrogant at all costs.

We must have equal status at seated meetings too. So if we are presenting to a seated audience round a boardroom table and we stand up to speak, then our status has changed. Physically we are saying, for this moment, I am more important than you. So what we need to do, is to redress the balance of status.

But what do most people do when they stand to present?

They get louder. Which only reinforces the unequal status.

We should actually get a little quieter when we stand. It's counter-intuitive I know, but we don't need a huge amount of volume when we present in a boardroom.

It's really important that we keep the status between us and our audience equal at all times if we want to connect with them.

4. No mixed messages

When we meet someone for the first time and we shake their hand, we're literally reaching out the hand of human friendship. We are not exposing ourselves unwisely. We are merely giving two pieces of information: That we wish to engage in some sort of communication and that we are happy to be doing this.

But many of us, even in this simple act of greeting, manage to cloud the issue. I once described someone as having a 'fuzzy politeness' - a classic mixed message, seeming to be polite but possibly doing it for the wrong reasons. We want clarity not fuzziness.

I remember reading a review of a politician who was described as having a mixture of 'ingratiation, anger and forced jollity'.

It's this mixture of messaging that gets in the way of clear communication. We are unlikely to invite someone in their Zone Two if we are giving them mixed signals. None of us trust mixed signals - they make us run for the hills.

When we meet someone for the first time in a business situation, we generally give our name and our job title. Our name is a fact. If we hate our name it is not the fault of the person we're meeting. We shouldn't pass on our insecurities to them. And our job title is also a fact. Again if we are unhappy with our job title it is not the fault of the person we are meeting.

Let me give you an example. A few years ago, my wife invited a couple round for dinner. I had never met the man before and whilst pouring him a drink, I asked what line of work he was in. It seemed a reasonable opening, and possibly less innocuous than discussing the weather.

These are the words he said in reply, 'I am Area Manager for a paper company. I should have been Chairman by now. But please don't judge me too harshly.' My heart sank as I thought of the long evening stretching ahead of me.

In fact, of course, he didn't say that. What he actually said was, 'I am Area Manager for a paper company.' The rest was said by his body language. His body was mass of subtle twitches, suggesting an enormous chip on his shoulder, resulting in somebody who was appearing to be full of self-judgement and unhappy with his situation.

By giving mixed messages he was coming across as less confident than I suspect he probably was. His body language had given the game away.

Self-judgement often leads to us into giving mixed messages. If we judge ourselves during our actual presentation we can't be focussing on our message or the audience. So those ringing questions in our heads are really unhelpful, 'Am I doing this OK? Have I prepared well enough? Do they understand my talk?'

If we listen to these thoughts, we will almost certainly end up giving the audience mixed messages.

We can never be saying one thing and thinking another. That will inevitably come across as a mixed message.

We are all aware of corporate brands. We visit a company website and immediately the design, colour scheme and font make us feel a particular way about that company. Their branding is clear. It goes across their advertising, their product range, right through to the way they answer the telephone. In other words their brand is always 'consistent'.

Think back to the teachers you had when you were at school. What children (and adults) like are clear and consistent boundaries. We like to know where we stand with someone - every day. It is difficult for a child when a teacher is strict one day and lenient the next. Teachers without consistent boundaries have no sense of their own brand. And without a clear sense of our own brand, people don't know who we are, what we stand for or how to interact with us.

If your brand is crystal clear to you, you will begin to radiate your brand with no mixed messages. And if your brand is consistent, your customers, colleagues and friends will know you, recommend you and love you for who you really are.

The actor Dennis Hopper had clearly thought about his brand when he said, 'James Dean said "I need you", Marlon Brando said "Screw you", and I'm somewhere in between.'

When I ask my clients what their brand is, they often reply 'I am CEO of X Corporation', despite the fact that they may also be a husband, a father or a keen sportsman. It seems that, in some sense, they have 'become their job'.

And if they have become their job, we know nothing about them as a human being. And audiences, of course, are made up of human beings. They have highs and lows, happiness and sadness. Indeed, they have all arrived in different emotional states. Some will be happy, maybe having just bought a new house or fallen in love, and some will be feeling vulnerable, maybe having had a failed relationship or suffered a recent bereavement. If we want to connect with every member of an audience, we must be aware of these different emotional states. The people in the audience who are feeling 'vulnerable' that day may well respond better to a CEO that also comes across as a balanced human being rather than simply being a corporate face.

Try to recall some of the great speakers you've heard. They will have seemed more interested in their ideas and in their audience and less concerned with themselves. These great speakers have managed somehow to reconnect with the childlike wonder and inquisitiveness which makes you immediately want to listen to them and to be around them.

So how do we remember what we were like as a young child?

I recently came across an old black and white photo of me on a donkey on Blackpool beach. I tried to imagine what I might have been thinking and feeling as I sat there in my little saddle.

I wrote down a list of five words that described me at that age.

Then I wrote down five words that I'd like people to think about me now.

Try this for yourself, it's a fascinating exercise. See if the two lists are in any way similar.

Interestingly, when I ask my clients to do this, the word that generally comes up first is 'professional'. Other popular words include charismatic, confident, knowledgeable, engaging, empathetic, trustworthy and efficient. Most people put either confident or professional at the top of their list.

We must have a very clearly defined sense of who we are at all times, so that our audience can really hear our message.

On my step-daughter's bedroom wall is a poster with the slogan:

YOU ARE BORN UNIQUE,
DON'T DIE A COPY.

We are all born unique. We are all born special. It doesn't make us better or more important than anybody else. But it does make us 'US'.

So let's learn to be 'ourselves' and not cloud our communication with mixed messages.

5. Don't justify

In my early days as an actor, when auditioning for a play, I would often catch myself 'justifying' why they should give me the job.

If the particular play was a comedy, I would list my entire CV of comedy parts. If it was a tragedy, I would tell them everything tragic that had happened in my life.

But once I realised that 'less is more' when it comes to justifying yourself in interviews, I was much more successful in getting jobs.

So when a director asked, 'Do you think you can play this role?' 'Yes, I think I can,' is a much better answer than, 'Yes, I think I can because I played in a comedy last year that went really well and I've just done a comedy on TV where I got great reviews …' etc., etc. Trying too hard. Trying to justify. Not good. Especially when it's delivered too fast.

The same is true when presenting an argument in a talk. A speaker who is desperate to justify or prove they have the answer will often just look desperate.

What often happens, when someone disagrees with us, is that we insist they come round to our way of thinking. And the more we push and insist, the more they will fight it.

So we must get into the mind-set that we have don't have to justify our argument. Assuming we have done our research and have made a well reasoned case, we simply have to present it.

Whether we are selling or motivating, it will be much more effective if we just say it, we don't have to justify it.

6. Listening

'Nature hath given men one tongue but two ears, that we may hear from others twice as much as we speak.' (Epictetus)

If we want to encourage our audience into their Zone Two, then it's vital that we listen to them. If we talk non-stop, without allowing time and space for them to join in, they will eventually give up trying to listen and all channels of communication will be closed down. Even if we don't actually want a response, we should check to see that they are still engaged.

When we meet someone new and they tell us their name, it's up to us to listen to it carefully.

People often tell me that they can't remember names - unlike the Rev. Spooner, who famously said, 'I remember your name perfectly, but I just can't think of your face.' But assuming that the person said their name clearly, we still have to listen actively to hear it.

By listening and showing an interest in them, we will encourage our audience to join us in their Zone Two. We will encourage them to have a conversation and communicate with us.

Giving a talk should feel like a conversation. It may well be that you speak for half an hour without interruption but it should still feel like a two-way exchange.

We must allow the audience time to process the information we give. Their 'silent listening' is their part of the conversation.

If we told our friends about a recent holiday and they didn't interrupt for five minutes, it would have effectively become a five minute 'speech'.

Their 'silent listening' is their part of the conversation. They would still feel involved because we have allowed them time to listen and to process the information.

We haven't been talking *at* them, we have been having a conversation *with* them.

By listening we will encourage our audience to join us in their Zone Two.

7. Eye contact

Imagine you have just met someone at a party. How many seconds should you hold eye contact for? I am assuming that this is not someone that you wish to date but a regular meeting. Two seconds? Three seconds? Twenty seconds?

It's a trick question, of course. There is no set amount of time. It depends on many factors. But mostly it depends on the other person and how comfortable they are with holding eye contact. It's about them. As we have already established, all communication is about them. It's never about you.

But if we had to suggest an amount of time, the answer is probably around two or three seconds.

But what about when you're giving a talk? If you are speaking to three or four people it's pretty easy to have eye contact with them as you present around a boardroom table. But what about when speaking in a larger hall to twenty people, or over a hundred? You can't see all their faces or their eyes. So how do you hold eye contact for two or three seconds with every single one of them?

What most of us do is to sweep the room. Possibly even de-focussing so that we can't see the audience clearly. We almost deliberately make them appear blurred, which can seem less frightening.

Many people say they get distracted if they see someone yawning, and assume they must be boring the audience, so they start to speed up.

I went to see *Hamlet* at the National Theatre in London a few years ago and was lucky enough to get a seat on the front row, bang in the centre. There was a pause and I knew the big 'To be or not to be?' speech was coming up. These lines are so famous that most actors feel they should deliver them in an interesting or unique way. Rather like an actress playing Lady Bracknell in *The Importance of Being Earnest* having to say the famous line, 'A handbag?'

So there I was, desperate to see how this actor would deliver one of the most famous lines in Shakespeare. After a pause, the actor walked down to front of the stage very slowly, looked me straight in the eye and said, 'To be or not be?' He stayed there, looking straight at me, waiting for my response.

I should say at this point that I didn't know the actor playing Hamlet personally. He must have chosen someone at random in the centre of the front row every night to deliver those famous lines to.

After a long pause he continued, 'That's the question.' I felt I almost wanted to say, 'Look, Hamlet, if you want to kill yourself, mate, that's up to you, but I can't have your death on my conscience.'

Afterwards I met a friend of mine and said, 'It's amazing, I was sitting in the front row and he played it all to me.' My friend said, 'He can't have done because I was in the dress circle and he played it all to me.'

What is interesting, of course, is that he hadn't played it all to me. He had only said those two lines to me, admittedly two of the most famous lines in Shakespeare, but what I had said to my friend was, 'He played it all to me.' So I was left with the feeling that it had all been played to me. And so had my friend, who had also only had two lines played directly to him.

So that's the secret of eye contact. One thought with one person and one thought with another. Now, of course, the actor could see me on the front row but probably not my friend in the dress circle, with the stage lights shining in his eyes. But he had directed his thoughts to a very specific area of the theatre each time. One thought here. One thought there. All around the auditorium, so by the end of the play everyone felt Hamlet had been talking specifically to them at some point.

We can do the same in a large hall when giving a talk or a presentation. Direct one thought to one area and one thought to another.

Even in a smaller boardroom situation, where you'd be able to see their eyes, don't be tempted to sweep the table. Have one thought with one person and one thought with another.

By using your eye contact in this way, your audience will feel that you are talking to them individually. No-one wants to feel they are just part of the crowd. We all want to feel special.

Damien Hirst said, 'My audience is one person.' If we remember that, we stand a better chance of connecting with every member of the audience individually.

Of course, in a one to one setting continuous full on direct eye contact can become uncomfortable.

Ask a friend to say three sentences to you about their last holiday. Watch what they are doing with their eyes as they speak. Do they hold continuous eye contact with you or do their eyes dart around your face or the room as they are thinking about their next sentence?

As you listen, try looking at both of their eyes at the same time. Of course, it's impossible, so instead look from one eye to another. Do this gently, moving from one to the other. It will look as if you really are listening. Ask your friend to do the same thing back you. It should feel as if they are listening to you even more intently.

You can also scan the bridge of their nose, their cheekbones or their forehead to give you break time from direct eye-to-eye contact.

Be careful not to move below the nose as lingering on the mouth could signal mating interest (unless that is your intention, of course).

8. Give them the choice to agree or disagree

Imagine you walked into my furniture shop, wanting to buy a chair and I said, 'Have a look around. Please buy any chair you want, but if you ask me, I would choose this one. And I would choose this one because it's the only chair in the shop that's green - it's environmentally friendly. But please buy any chair you like.'

There are three very basic sales techniques on show here to encourage you to at least consider the 'green' chair.

1. As I run a chair shop my personal recommendation has some credibility - I probably know more about chairs than you do.
2. I gave you an emotional, environmental reason to choose the 'green' one.
3. I gave you the choice to decide for yourself which chair to buy.

The freedom to decide for yourself is the most important one here. We didn't like being told what to think as children and we like it even less as adults.

If I want to encourage you to buy this chair it is important that I don't sound like I am *selling* it. You will only think it's the best chair in the world if I sound like I believe it myself. If I know it's the best chair, I don't have to prove it. And at the same time, I give you the absolute right to disagree with me.

So when you are giving a talk, your tone of voice and the choice of words you use must always be slanted towards letting the audience decide for themselves.

Aristotle says that, ideally, an audience should get to the final conclusion a moment before, or at the same time as, the speaker does. They want to feel that they have come to their conclusions themselves.

That is why a 'lecturing' tone doesn't work well. Of course, there are many brilliant lecturers out there, but here I'm talking about the worst sort of lecturing tone; one that sounds controlling and loud. It is relentless and insistent and does not allow us to decide for ourselves.

At best, we won't like it. At worst, we will switch off.

9. Don't take yourself too seriously

'Never trust a man who, when left alone in a room with a tea cosy, doesn't try it on.' Billy Connolly

When we see a speaker who takes themselves too seriously or is too full of themselves, we can't wait for them to slip on the proverbial banana skin.

If their lectern falls over, I assure you we will laugh. And rightly so, because they have set themselves up for a fall. We feel they deserve our ridicule and we feel justified in laughing.

Agatha Christie once said, 'It's a curious thought - but it's only when you see people looking ridiculous that you realize how much you love them.'

Perhaps we should bear that in mind. I'm not suggesting clown outfits or spinning bow ties, but a healthy slice of self-deprecating humour can go a long way.

Let's try to develop a sense of humour about ourselves.

It should look as if we're enjoying being up there. If it looks as if we're taking ourselves too seriously or facing a firing squad, then there's very little chance that the audience will enjoy the experience either.

If we take ourselves too seriously we could come across as self-important or pompous - both are Zone Three behaviours.

10. Smile

Nothing you wear is more important than your smile. It makes the audience feel that you are relaxed and want to be there.

Again, I'm not talking about a false toothpaste commercial smile, I'm talking about a twinkle in the eyes.

It's not always appropriate to smile, of course, and in some situations it would be completely wrong. But most of us could smile much more than we do when we speak in public.

Remember that smiling is easy - it's easier than looking serious.

In fact, it takes 42 muscles to frown but only 17 to smile.

One of my drama teachers told a class, 'If you don't know how to say a line, say it dirty.' I'm not sure I'd necessarily recommend that but if you did, it would at least make you smile.

But I should offer a word of warning here - smiling is an aggressive sign in chimpanzees. Your audience is not usually made up of chimpanzees, but if you ever find yourself speaking to a room full of chimpanzees, you have been warned.

American actress and coach Dorothy Sarnoff recommends smiling rather than what she calls 'executive neutral'.

Let's try to avoid executive neutral during your talk.

Try smiling instead.

EXERCISE 1

Observe which Zones other people are in

Observe at least three people you meet today. Try to work out which Communication Zone they are in. You can try this with your family, work colleagues or strangers.

If we know which Zones other people are in, then we can then learn to adapt our behaviour and encourage them to move into their Zone Two.

So initially, just observe which Zone they are in. See how quickly you can spot their Zones. Learning to spot which Zone other people are in will become automatic after a while.

Once you've learned to spot which Zones other people are in, observe how you feel when you are talking to someone who is in their Zone One, Two or Three.

How do they make you feel by being where they are? Their choice of Zone will directly affect the way you feel towards them.

EXERCISE 2

Observe which Zones you are in

Now take a look at yourself. Which Zone are you in right now? Most people tend to have a favourite Zone, or at least a favourite Zone for certain situations.

So which Zones have you been in today? One, Two or Three? Observe yourself. Have you changed in and out of different Zones during the day?

Do you find yourself being drawn to particular people today? Particular people in particular Zones?

If you are in Zone One, you are unlikely to want to spend time with people in Zone Three. They will probably be too loud and controlling and make you feel under attack.

If you are in Zone Three, you may be irritated by the lack of energy of people in Zone One.

But if you are in Zone Two, you probably won't find people either annoying or threatening.

EXERCISE 3

Try actively choosing your Zones

Do you find yourself wanting to change your Zone depending on which Zone other people are in?

Start by being in Zone One. This will be fairly easy and non-threatening to other people. (Of course, if you wake up in Zone Three today, you might find this a little harder.)

Then try having a conversation with someone while you are in your Zone Two. You'll be open and welcoming, you'll take time to listen and make other people feel you're genuinely interested in them. You can still have your opinions, of course, but you will listen carefully, trying not to talk over them.

And now try a conversation in Zone Three. Choose someone neutral, someone to whom the outcome doesn't matter so much. Try asking for help in a shop you don't normally go into or asking for directions from a stranger whilst being in your Zone Three. (Close friends and colleagues might take offense and ask if you're OK today if they are not used to your being in Zone Three. Let's not upset anyone too close to you unnecessarily.)

How did it make you feel when you were in different Zones?

How did others react to you when you were in different Zones? Did they change their behaviour depending on which Zone you were in?

Recognising which Zone we are currently in, and which Zone our audience is in, helps us move to that perfect space where both our Zone Twos overlap - where communication can flow freely and openly.

3

Your nerves

Over two thousand years ago, the young Cicero suffered from terrible nerves. He wrote, 'Personally, I am always very nervous when I begin to speak. Every time I make a speech I feel I am submitting to judgement, not only about my ability but my character and honour. I am afraid of seeming either to promise more than I can perform, which suggests complete irresponsibility, or to perform less than I can, which suggests bad faith and indifference.'

He later studied with tutors from academia and the theatre to become one of Rome's greatest orators.

The 3rd US President, Thomas Jefferson, would probably struggle to get elected today. He was not made for the television age, his voice was high-pitched and he spoke with a lisp. This wouldn't have worked in today's 'sound-bite' culture. It's no surprise to learn then that he intensely disliked public speaking. He despised giving speeches so much that he sent his State of the Union addresses to Congress by letter rather than delivering them himself in person.

British Prime Minister, Benjamin Disraeli, was a skilled wordsmith but his early speeches were disastrous. He failed to get elected four times for three different parties. Eventually he found his political voice, of course, but it took him a while.

Winston Churchill was so nervous during his maiden speech at the House of Commons that he actually fainted.

Many great speakers have had difficult times in the early stages of their career. They weren't all born with the confidence and charisma that we associate with them now. They learned their skills, dared to take a few risks and started on their journey to become great speakers.

So let us start to take a few gentle (albeit risky) steps on our speaking journey - for as playwright Neil Simon said, 'If no-one ever took risks, Michelangelo would have painted the Sistine floor'.

Today, it's really important that we can all speak well. We all have stories to tell, people to sell to or people to motivate. Some of us do this in the public eye on the world stage and some of us do it more quietly in private rooms but we all do have to communicate. So let's learn to become successful speakers. And we can - it's really not that difficult.

I don't like the way I look

Before we even climb the steps to the rostrum to give a talk, many of us have to face our own personal insecurities.

If we don't like the way we look and are worried that we are too old, too young, too fat or too thin, then we feel doubly exposed when we stand up to speak in public.

John Wilkes, who invented the free press, was by all accounts not a handsome fellow, but he spoke with great passion. He said, 'I can talk away my face in twenty seconds.' His audience stopped judging him and started listening because he had come to terms with his looks.

If our message is well constructed and we deliver it with energy, clarity and humanity, then our audience will very quickly stop judging us physically and start to listen to what we are saying.

Some of the most beautiful people I have ever met have not necessarily been classically beautiful. But they appear to have a real beauty. They often have a sparkle deep within their eyes. When you meet someone like that, what you notice is the spirit inside them.

It may be worth remembering that many people in the audience aren't particularly in love with their faces or their bodies either.

I once played the lead in a play in London where I had to appear nude for five minutes at the end of Act One. That's right - totally nude. I was worried, of course, as any of us would be about standing there in our birthday suit, but I'm sure most people sat in the audience thinking 'I'm glad it's not me up there!' But do you know what? After a couple of seconds, despite standing there in my altogether, the audience started to listen to what I was saying.

After appearing nude, public speaking was never quite so daunting again. I'm not sure that I would recommend being that drastic but as John Wilkes said, if you speak with passion the audience will very soon forget what you look like and will start to listen to what you have to say.

But even if we get over the way we look, we may still face the speaker's ultimate nightmare - nerves.

Dealing with nerves

So there you are, standing up in front of a group of people, and your muscles start to shake, you feel sick, you can't remember a word, your mouth goes dry, you can't swallow and your voice stops working. Not great, is it? Why does this happen?

Back in the days when we were living in caves and being attacked by wild animals, our bodies sent panic alarms to the neural pathways in the oldest part of the brain, the amygdala. This is what we call the fight or flight response. The brain is often unable to judge the severity of the danger and often responds to fear disproportionally. So whether we are being attacked by a dinosaur or facing fifty people from a podium, the brain sends the same eight signals along those ancient neural pathways. These signals, the eight fight or flight responses, tell us either to fight or to run. We probably won't try to either fight or run from our audience but the brain keeps on sending those ancient signals anyway. And it's those ancient signals that make us respond to nerves in the ways we know all too well.

Let's look at those eight responses.

1. At times of life threatening danger the brain actually downgrades the importance of its own functions. Actually running away is far more important than thinking about running away. People who have done heroic acts in dangerous situations often say afterwards, 'I don't remember much about it - it was all just a blur.'

2. The brain sends a message to the heart, to increase the blood flow so that it can send oxygen and adrenalin via the blood supply to our legs and arms to fight or to run. So our heart rate and blood pressure instantly rise.

But if blood is being syphoned off to the legs and arms, where do we now have a vastly reduced flow of blood?

That's right - in the brain. When the body goes into fight or flight mode, we often feel light-headed, resulting in our forgetting our words or, as in Churchill's case, actually fainting.

3. A message is then sent to the lungs. We'll need more oxygen if we are to fight or run, so we'll need to increase our breathing rate. But as we are giving a speech and not using up this extra oxygen we can end up hyperventilating, again feeling light-headed and faint.

4. The brain sends adrenalin to our eyes, so we can find an escape route. You can often see a speaker's eyes darting around the room wildly or looking slightly startled. We can even behave like the child who says: 'If I can't see the dinosaur, then the dinosaur can't see me.' It might be sensible to avoid eye contact with an aggressive dinosaur, but we shouldn't let our subconscious make us feel the audience is out to kill us.

5. There's a small chance that the dinosaur hasn't seen us, so to protect us the brain cuts off our voice box. Now we can't speak. Nothing will come out of our mouths - it's similar to the effect of a silent scream in a dream when you shout and nothing will come out.

6. We don't want to choke on our own saliva as we run, so the brain stops producing saliva, so we now have a dry throat and mouth.

7. The brain sends signals to draw blood away from the stomach - there is no time to digest food as the blood is now needed to give your muscles extra fire power. This can often leave us feeling sick - not great for after dinner speakers.

8. You are standing up in front of your audience, in full fight or flight mode, and the body is sending ancient chemical signals urging your body to run but you are about

to give a speech and you can't run. The muscles become so overloaded with oxygen and adrenalin that they simply cannot stand still. Eventually they will start running on their own.

This is the physiological reason why we shake. It's not because we are at fault or because we are somehow being weak or pathetic, it is because we are human and we are responding as any human being (or indeed any animal) does to a perceived threat - we stay and fight, or we run away.

So those are the eight signals that the brain sends out when it responds to a perceived threat.

Understanding this can help us realise that our fear responses are not a failing in us, but are simply a protective animal response. A response that every other human 'animal' will have at such moments of perceived threat.

What we, as speakers, have to do is to learn how to cope with these responses. We have to learn how to use all that adrenalin to our advantage.

Dale Carnegie says that 'fear only exists in the mind'. It does but when we feel it, we still have to face these eight physical responses. In a moment, I'll suggest some tips to deal with our responses to those signals.

Let's first look at our fears around giving a talk.

Dealing with fears

Apart from nerves on the day, we can also have brooding fears about our upcoming talk.

There are two types of fears:
internal fears - how we respond personally, and
external fears - caused by things that we feel are outside our control.

The five most common **internal** fears are:

1. Fear of forgetting our words

Fear of forgetting our words or going off script is, of course, a worry for many professional speakers, actors and singers. But if you are giving a presentation, most of the audience will not know what you had intended to say anyway. So if you forget your words, or go off script, they probably won't even be aware of it.

2. Fear of being judged

We often think the whole audience is sitting there judging us and we spend time worrying what others will think of us. But remember that audiences have their own issues to worry about; they'll often tune in and out of your speech thinking about their own day-to-day worries. They might very well not even notice if you blushed for a short while or that your hand shook for a couple of seconds.

3. Fear of large audiences

A client said to me the other day, 'It's ok if I can see their eyes but if I can't see their faces it's like being in front of a firing squad.'

I often ask clients at what number does the size of an audience become frightening. 5? 10? 20? 50? 100? 500?

For most people it's when they can't see the audience clearly anymore.

Under that number we can see their eyes and their faces and read how we're doing. But in bigger groups we often treat the audience as one huge mass - as one huge dinosaur - and we want to run for the caves. We must try to remember that an audience is made up of a series of individuals.

4. Fear of panicking

People often say, 'My talk went badly last time, so it's bound to go even worse this time.' But remember that today is not yesterday; as Lewis Carol said, 'I can't go back to yesterday because I was a different person then.'

And even if it did go badly last time there might have been specific reasons that caused that. In this book we will hopefully anticipate all the possible causes, so that next time your talk will go brilliantly.

5. Fear of looking nervous

Some people also have a fear of not only being nervous but looking nervous. 'If they can see me shaking, they'll think I am nervous, and then I become even more nervous - it's a vicious circle.' Fear not, at the end of this chapter there are some specific exercises to help with this challenge.

Then there are **external** fears. The seven most common ones are:

1. The importance of the outcome of the speech.

2. The size and composition of the audience.

3. The venue - is it somewhere you know, like your own board room, or an unknown conference centre?

4. The time of day - some people are better in the morning and get nervous waiting till later in the day to give their talk and others are more relaxed in the evening.

5. Your own state of wellbeing. What is going on in your life? This, of course, can have a huge effect on the way we anticipate giving a talk.

6. The audience's reaction - if we see one person yawning we tend to think that they are all bored. But it might just be that that one person didn't get much sleep the night before.

7. And sometimes, as Franklin D. Roosevelt said, 'The only thing we have to fear, is fear itself.'

It is perfectly natural for us to feel a little nervous before giving a speech - professional performers feel that too - but we should also allow ourselves a little dose of adrenalin, it can up our excitement factor. What we don't want is for the nerves and the fears to pull us out of control. We must remember that this it not actually a life and death situation, even though the body might be responding as if it were.

We've seen speakers whose hands have shaken when holding their notes. They often end up gripping the lectern, if there is one, to try to stop the shaking. Then their voice starts to wobble. And the feeling of panic takes over. I know what that feels like. We all do.

Top tip of the day

How can we stop our body from shaking when we feel nervous?

There is a very simple answer to this. And it's far simpler than you can imagine.

It is almost physically impossible to shake if you squeeze your buttocks or your thighs.

I don't mean squeeze them with your hands, of course; I mean clench the muscles themselves. I promise you it will stop the shaking.

Why does clenching our buttocks or our thighs work so well? To answer that question we should look back at our eight fight or flight responses.

There are four benefits to clenching your buttocks or your thighs.

1. The brain is sending signals to our legs and arms to run and when we don't run the muscles will soon become over-flowing with oxygen and adrenalin demanding that we do run.

But we're on stage about to give a speech and we can't run, even if we'd like to. So eventually the muscles in our legs and arms over-power our own self-will and they start moving on their own. They just can't ignore these chemical messages any longer and they start to shake. We try to keep them still but they keep trying to run and the more we try to stop them the more vigorously they shake.

By clenching our buttock or thigh muscles we are answering the chemical signals to contract the muscles and so, miraculously, we will stop shaking.

2. The more we clench them, the more we are squeezing blood back up to the brain. Because we're in fight or flight mode, the brain has devalued itself and diverted most of the blood to the important leg and arm muscles. But by squeezing we are causing the veins to contract which sends blood back up to the brain. So now we are less likely to feel light-headed or forget our words.

3. By clenching our buttocks or thighs we are taking away any tension we might have had in the chest and throat areas. This is where most speakers tighten up during a talk. If we can focus all our tension into the bigger thigh or buttock muscles, then we are releasing the chest and throat areas so we can free our voice.

4. By clenching our thighs we add one further benefit. Probably the most valuable of all: you should know this one by now.

Clenching our buttocks or our thighs lowers our centre of gravity. And if we lower our centre of gravity we will feel more centred and more confident.

So there are four huge benefits to clenching your buttocks or your thighs.

And, of course, there is a fifth benefit.

Well, more of a side benefit really. You could end up with very firm buttocks or thighs - but I'll leave that one with you ...

Knowing how you will start your talk

In Chapter 6 (Your Structure) we will look at different ways to start your talk, to grab the audience's attention from the very beginning.

Once you know exactly what your first words will be, you'll begin to feel less nervous before you start and more confident as you speak.

Knowing how you will end your talk

And when you know exactly how you will end your talk, having planned it properly, you will gain even more confidence, knowing that it won't just fizzle out.

Let's take all the elements of chance out of the equation so you'll feel less nervous.

Now you know how to keep centred and keep tension away from your throat.

You'll have planned exactly what you are going to say at the start and exactly what you are going to say at the end.

You'll begin to look and feel much better as you first approach the platform, so your audience's *blink* will be 'confident'.

Knowing how you will stand

In Chapter 5 (Your Body Language) we will look at the many different ways you can stand as you deliver your talk.

As always with public speaking, there are many ways and styles of delivering your talk. But there will probably be a right way for you to stand - a way that makes you feel and look comfortable and centred.

Once you have found a way of standing that works for you, once you know what you'll do with your hands and how you'll hold your notes, then many of your nerves will naturally disappear.

Here are three exercises that are great for dealing with nerves and tension - experiment with these now.

You can also do them just before you give your talk.

EXERCISE 1

Push a wall

Stand normally and say this nursery rhyme out loud:

Humpty Dumpty sat on a wall,
Humpty Dumpty had a great fall.
All the King's horses,
And all the King's men
Couldn't put Humpty together again!

Now stand and face a wall. Place both hands on the wall about shoulder height and push really hard, as if you're trying to push the wall a couple of meters in the direction you're pushing.

This is a great exercise for releasing tension in the upper chest. It frees your voice and helps relax any nervous tension.

Now, after pushing a wall, stand normally and try saying *Humpty Dumpty* again. See how much more relaxed you feel and open you sound.

EXERCISE 2

Push your hands together

Sit straight upright in a chair.

Put your hands together as in prayer. Make sure your forearms are parallel to the ground. Gently relax and part your lips. Breathe in.

Now push your hands together as hard as you can.

As you push, squeeze the air from your lungs out through your mouth.

This releases tension in the upper chest and also engages the diaphragm 'triangle' as you push your air out.

EXERCISE 3

Beating rising nerves

If you find your heart racing and have a sense of rising panic before you are about to speak, try this exercise.

You can do this even when people are watching you. So if you have to sit on a stage waiting to speak, in full view of the audience, this is one for you.

Breathe in through your nose very slowly for a count of three.

Then breathe out though your nose for a count of three.

Repeat this three times.

That should take you a total of 18 seconds. In that time you will have significantly lowered your heart rate.

Try this one even if your heart is not racing. It will centre you and will feel rather like you have had a short meditation. Your mind will be calmer, you will speak more slowly and your voice will be more centred.

4

Your Voice

'The voice is the muscle of the soul.'   (Roy Hart)

The human body has five senses: touch, taste, sight, smell and hearing. The two most developed senses are sight and hearing. So let's make sure that the visual and vocal messages that we send out are the best they can be.

The more work I do with clients, the more I believe that our voice is one of the most important communication tools we have; as important as the visual signals we give out and the content we deliver.

The BBC undertook some research into the power of radio in the 1930s with two groups of people. Each group was given the same information but one group read it for themselves and the other group had it read to them by an announcer. The group that had read it for themselves were found to be much more critical of the information than those that had had it read to them. The human voice, when used properly, can often have more authority than the written word.

From bedtime stories as young children right through to adults in a business meeting, we feel safe and we believe speakers who have confident, relaxed and warm voices.

Our voice creates an impression, either good or bad, whether we like it or not. We use our voices all the time - not just when giving a talk or a presentation. Our voices say something about us in everyday life too, in a shop and on the phone. People respond to warm, confident voices - they seem friendly and command respect.

Speaking for any length of time requires vocal energy, stamina and passion. A speaker needs to have a relaxed, expressive and engaging voice.

We can develop our ability to speak clearly, and our range of vocal expression, by working on breathing and articulation exercises. There are some exercises at the end of this chapter to help us relax and work on our voice.

Many people have developed bad vocal habits, from speaking too fast with a monotonous tone to mumbling and dropping the ends of their sentences. On top of all this, when standing up and speaking in public, we also have to face the prospect of nerves affecting our voice.

An audience can't listen easily to us if they feel nervous for us so it's really important to overcome nerves when we present.

One of the reasons we get nervous when speaking in public is that the voice coming out of our mouth often isn't our usual voice.

It's a different voice.

Nerves and the pressure of having to give a talk can pull us off centre and our voice can sound 'odd' to us. As a result we begin to feel 'odd' ourselves.

And if we don't feel we're being ourselves then, of course, we get more nervous and want this out-of-body experience to stop.

Use your own voice

You might well say, 'Of course I'm going to use my own voice. Who else's voice am I going to use?'

But many of us have different voices that we use on different occasions. We have a telephone voice. A public speaking voice. A voice for our children. A voice for our lover. A voice for our parents. We have listening voice, a kind voice, an understanding and an empathetic voice, an authoritative voice and an angry voice. Some of us have a different voice when we speak to foreigners, to people in authority over us or to those who look up to us.

If we can learn to find our 'own' voice, rather than using a 'public speaking' voice, we will feel that we are authentically being ourselves and so will our audience.

There are some people who always seem to use the same voice. Try to think of somebody you know who uses the same voice all the time. How do they make you feel when they speak with you? These people usually have a strong sense of who they are. The rest of us, chameleon-like, often change our voice depending on the situation. This can make us appear lightweight and un-centred.

Your emotional centre

Where, in your body, is your emotional centre?

Don't think about it, just point to somewhere on your body. Some people tell me they don't really understand the question, that they can't grasp the idea of even having an emotional centre. They say they simply feel emotions when and where they feel them. But if pushed they will probably choose one of these 5 areas: head, throat, heart, solar plexus or diaphragm.

Where do you think your emotional centre is?

People who choose their head, say that they process information and emotion in their head or their brain and therefore that must be their emotional centre.

Those who choose their throat suggest that's where they are affected most when they are nervous or upset.

Those who choose their heart say it's because we talk about having a broken heart. Poets write achingly about the affairs of the heart, so many people think that their emotional centre must be there. But I'm not sure that you feel anything in your heart, unless you have angina. You can feel your heart rate going up, of course, but that is not quite the same thing.

Some people suggest the solar plexus or diaphragm. If you have a high emotional response to a situation, your breathing rate changes. People talk of feeling winded or hyperventilated when under pressure.

The truth is that none of these is your emotional centre.

And, yes, all human beings have the same emotional centre.

Any thoughts yet?

The answer is lower. Much lower. The lower stomach, below your belly button. Your gut.

We speak of having a gut feeling. We get butterflies there, both if we are happy or if we are sad. Those feelings are then sent around the body to be processed in the head; they will affect your heart and your breathing rate and often result in a tightness in the throat, but all emotions initially start from your gut.

Why is this important?

Very simply, if we speak from our emotional centre, our gut, we will sound believable and come across as being ourselves. We will eventually make the actual sound from our throat, of course, but if the initial thought starts from a feeling in our gut, before we actually speak, it will be more believable. If the thought starts from our head or in our throat, there is what we call an 'emotional disconnect'. The voice transmits the words but they can sound empty and hollow. They are not connected to our emotional centre.

We all know the difference between a salesperson who is genuinely offering help and one who is trying to 'sell' us something with a false voice and a cheesy smile. But when we stand up to speak we want to come across as believable, honest and genuine.

Speak from your emotional centre

The next time you see a speaker, watch very carefully before they speak. If they breathe into their upper chest, the sound that comes out of their mouth will almost certainly be tight. It will be the sound of a teacher telling us off. I have often sat in an auditorium listening to a corporate speech and wondering why I was being told off, when all I had done was turn up to listen.

If, instead of speaking from our throat, we can learn to speak from our stomach, the results will be transformational. When we do this, we are using our 'natural' voice.

So if we can learn to lower our centre of gravity, we will begin to be able to speak from our emotional centre, our gut, and we'll begin to sound more like ourselves again.

Ultimately, we want the thought that starts from our emotional centre to produce a sound that comes up through the body and out through the throat with no interruption. Usually when we try to 'act' a thought, our audience will not believe us. What happens is that there's is an interruption in the thought between the lower stomach (our emotional centre) and the mouth - this interruption is usually in the throat area. The throat area becomes tight and is often constricted. Sometimes air comes out at the same time as the sound, reducing its impact.

Whether we are selling a product or an idea, we want to come across as 'believable' and 'real'. Any interruption in the throat area will not help our cause. Often the first understanding we have that a salesperson is not being honest is by the sound of their voice. Even if we haven't analysed where their voice is coming from, we know that the sound is not 'authentic' and as a result we don't believe them and probably won't buy their product or their idea.

We want our customers to believe us. If we are leading our team at work we want them to believe us, we want them to follow us on our journey. This can only happen if our voice starts in our emotional centre.

A few years ago, I was appearing in a British TV series, *Emmerdale*, set in Yorkshire. One day after filming I took the train back to London and sat in the 'quiet carriage'. This is a carriage where people can read, mobiles are supposed to be on silent and no music is allowed. Suddenly two teenage girls entered the carriage carrying a large ghetto blaster, clearly looking for an argument. They laughed as they banged the speaker system down on a table and turned the music up to a thumping volume. Most of the business people on their way home had clearly chosen the 'quiet carriage' for a reason. They didn't want the music but they also didn't want a fight.

I had been playing a policeman in the TV show and so was in 'policeman' mode. I decided the music should be turned off. And without a fight. I knew that I could only do this if I kept my centre of gravity low and used the power from my emotional centre.

I went up to the girls and said, 'Good evening, Ladies. The music is going off. That's not up for discussion - but would you like to do it the easy way or the hard way?' And do you know what? They tuned the music off and left the carriage. The rest of the carriage started applauding, which almost brought the girls back in again to start a full on fight. But I was delighted that speaking from my emotional centre had worked.

The sound of our own voice

Many people don't like hearing themselves back on a voice recorder or hearing their own greeting on their voice mail.

Why is this?

Firstly, our ears are behind our mouth, so we are used to hearing ourselves from 'behind', as it were. If we placed a microphone behind our head and recorded our voice, it might sound more like we are used to hearing it.

Secondly, we hear our voice via bone conduction and vibrations in our head, so it will inevitably have a different sound and feel when we hear it recorded.

Recording our own voice can be a helpful exercise because it is a more accurate version of what other people hear than how our voice sounds to us. It can tell us if we have enough vocal energy, variety and clarity as we speak.

Clarity not volume

'Nothing lowers the level of conversation more than raising the voice.' (Stanley Horowitz)

Most people not only use a different voice when they stand to speak in public, but they use a louder voice. Louder than is necessary.

I was constantly told at school to be louder. 'Speak up, lad. Don't be shy,' the teacher would say. That got me into the habit of being loud rather than simply being clear. When I went to drama college at the age of 18, I soon learned that 'clarity' was more important than 'volume'.

This is good news for clients who tell me that they are worried about having a 'quiet' voice. If they work on their clarity of speech, they usually find that their voice is quite loud enough. In any case, when we speak in a large hall we will usually have a microphone to provide the power.

We can all improve our voices by working on our articulation and clarity. Articulation is an old fashioned word for what our tongue is doing, the way it cuts up the words. Some people feel it is also an old fashioned concept. But if the audience can't hear our words, we might as well not say them in the first place.

Listening is hard work - especially at conferences, where audiences have to listen for many hours. They need the speaker's help to maintain their focus.

If we make it easy for the audience to hear us, they will listen.

I am a bit of a stickler for clear speech. We often hear a traffic announcer on the radio saying, 'There is bad congestion due to an earlier accident.' But many announcers will join words together, particularly when a word ends in an 'R'. So what we hear is, 'There is bad congestion due to an earlier raccident.' There is no such word as 'raccident'. Even my computer spell check is underlining it as I type. That is called an 'R liaison'. Try saying these words out loud, 'more ice'. It should not sound like 'more rice.'

And sometimes an 'R' creeps in when there shouldn't be one at all (an 'intrusive R') as in, 'I saw ra man.'

Of course, I'm aware that language is constantly changing and evolving, but the joining together of words that should ideally be separate always niggles me.

At the end of this chapter there are some articulation exercises for you to work on if you'd like to improve your clarity.

Our tongue is a muscle like any other and needs exercise. As you work on these exercises, imagine you are taking your tongue to the gym.

Don't change your voice when you stand up

Ideally we should use the same voice when we are standing up in public as we do when we are sitting down.

Most people can be heard and understood quite easily when sitting at a boardroom table and speaking at a normal volume. But when they stand to speak many people feel an extraordinary urge to start shouting. The size of the room has not changed but their volume has doubled.

There seems to be something about standing up in public that makes us feel we should get louder. Fight this urge.

If they can hear you when you are sitting down, they can hear you when you are standing up.

EXERCISE 1

The best tongue exercise in the world

One of the best ways to be vocally clear is to have an open throat and to get the tongue working properly. But when we get nervous, or when we are tired, the back of the throat can tighten up. The tongue can even feel as if it's being pulled backwards.

This exercise will help you open your throat.

I want you to stick your tongue out as far as you can and try to say the whole of *Humpty Dumpty*. (You might think this is an unusual request but I promise you it works.)

When I say I want you to stick your tongue out, I mean *really* stick it out and try to speak clearly. This will not work if you half stick it out, or if you don't *really* try to articulate.

Of course, it's hard to articulate with your tongue sticking out but by trying to speak as clearly as you can you are getting the back of the tongue to work harder. And by stretching the back of the tongue you will open the back of your throat.

So stick out your tongue out as far as you can and try to say clearly:

Humpty Dumpty sat on a wall,
Humpty Dumpty had a great fall.
All the King's horses,
And all the King's men
Couldn't put Humpty together again!

Once you have done that, try saying the whole of *Humpty Dumpty* again but this time speaking normally.

You should notice that you produce a more open sound. You may have also gained more depth, resonance and volume. Most people are amazed at how different their voice sounds immediately after doing this exercise.

As an actor, I 'voice' TV ads, documentaries and present live events, and I would never record one of these without first doing this exercise.

Training a voice can take many years. At Central School, where I trained as an actor, we did an hour of voice every day for three years. Of course, unless you want to go on the stage, you don't need your voice to work at the level of a professional actor. But ideally we should all have clear, relaxed and open voices. I recommend this exercise to almost every client and it really works.

How long do the effects of this exercise last?

Generally around five minutes. But the more you open the back of your throat by doing this exercise, the more the default position of your throat will become 'open'. If you were to do this exercise five or six times a day for a week, you would really begin to notice a difference. And if it became a daily exercise over time, you could transform your voice.

Counting from one to twenty has the same effect as saying *Humpty Dumpty* but there is something faintly ridiculous about this exercise, so I think it helps to be saying something faintly ridiculous too.

Try this exercise before making a telephone call. The person you are calling won't have seen you sticking your tongue out. Notice if your voice feels stronger and more open as you speak.

It is, without question, the simplest and the best single voice exercise in the world.

EXERCISE 2

Opening your throat

The *Humpy Dumpty* tongue exercise is great for opening your throat.

Here is another one. It is the 'half yawn'.

Stand facing a spot on the wall - a picture or a light switch works well. Breathe in, and on the outbreath say:

"Good morning, Ladies and Gentlemen.'

Now try to imagine you are about to yawn. Take in a wide 'yawny' breath and then say again:

'Good morning, Ladies and Gentlemen.'

Try this a few more times. It should begin to feel as though your throat is more open.

When you are out and about today, try this exercise. See how your voice feels when you start to speak.

You can even try this before entering a shop. This should release any tension in your throat. Remember you a trying to keep your throat open and relaxed.

EXERCISE 3

Centre your breath

Sit forward on a chair with your eyes gently closed. Put your hand on your lower stomach and, as you breathe in, try to breathe 'into' your hand. Try not to breathe into your upper chest but into your hand, almost as if you are making your stomach larger. So breathe into your hand and then breathe out.

Do this 3 times.

Now breathe in and, as you breathe out, make a gentle humming sound. Keep your jaw relaxed, with your lips closed so they tingle with the humming.

Also, do this 3 times.

Now breathe into your lower stomach again, and as you breathe out start making a humming sound for a couple of seconds, then open your lips and turn the humming sound into an 'Ahhh' sound. Don't be tempted to get loud.

Again, do this 3 times.

You should begin to feel that your breath and the sounds you make are starting in your lower stomach and then flowing freely out through your open throat.

The power of the breath comes from the lower stomach, while the throat remains open and relaxed.

EXERCISE 4

Centre your voice

Imagine you are an actor and a film script has just arrived in the post. You open it up and see that your first line of dialogue is:

'I love you. I hate you. I want to marry you. I want to kill you.'

Try speaking those sentences out loud now. As you say them, look at a spot on the wall.

Try not to 'act' them - if you act them, chances are they will sound false. Just try to say them neutrally.

Now say them again out loud and try to make each inflection the same. Imagine you are saying these sentences to someone who doesn't speak English. 'I love you' and 'I hate you' could sound the same to someone who doesn't understand the language.

Try saying these two sentences with the same inflection. 'I love you' and 'I hate you'. They may sound the same to you but the audience will get the difference.

Now try another exercise. Still talking to the same spot on the wall, say these famous lines from *Hamlet* quietly and gently:

'To be or not to be? That is the question.'

Don't 'act' it, just let the words flow from your lower stomach. It's as if the sound pours out from your open throat.

Your voice should not feel forced or pushed, it should simply flow from your lower stomach and carry your emotions that started in your emotional centre. It is actually very simple.

And now, Hey Presto, in one fell swoop you could play Hamlet.

The simplicity of this delivery should connect your voice to your emotional centre and will sound much more believable to your audience.

EXERCISE 5

Smiling changes your voice

Smiling really does change the sound of your voice. If you don't believe me, try recording yourself.

First, with a completely straight face record yourself saying this sentence:

'Good morning, Ladies and Gentlemen, I'm glad you've all turned up as I'd be feeling pretty stupid if I was standing here talking to myself.'

Now try recording the same sentence with a smile on your face as you speak.

As you listen back, you should find that the one with a smile in the voice is more engaging and has more energy and variation of tone.

I am not suggesting a TV game show host smile. I mean a slight smile - a twinkle in the eyes. I regularly ask clients to try their speech again with a slight smile. There are occasions when smiling is not appropriate, of course, but in most cases it will add energy and vocal range.

Try it, it really does change the way you sound and the way the audience will react.

EXERCISE 6

Observe your voice

Try observing yourself today. Listen to your voice. Try to notice when it is relaxed and when it is a little tighter. Does it depend on whom you're talking to? The importance of the situation? The level of other noise around? Is it easier or harder on the telephone?

For now just observe. Observe how it feels at different times. In which situations do you feel your voice tighten? When are you able to be more relaxed?

Once you've observed yourself in a few settings and scenarios, see if you can alter where your voice is coming from.

If you are speaking from your throat, and feel your voice is restricted, see if you can mentally shift your voice to your lower stomach. Use all the tools we have learned so far.

If you are about to make a phone call and you have some privacy, try the *Humpty Dumpty* tongue exercise or the half yawn to open your throat.

Try dropping the back of the tongue for a second - this will help release tension in the throat.

Try speaking a little more quietly. Check that you are not speaking too loudly - generally, when we speak on our throat, we get louder.

Observe your voice.

EXERCISE 7

Speaking from a low centre of gravity

Stand and clench your buttocks or your thighs, lowering your centre of gravity, and try to speak from your centre.

Say, gently and effortlessly:

'This is the best chair in the world.'

You are not trying to sell.

Just let the words flow gently out. You will find that you have more gravitas and will sound more confident and centred.

Try doing this when making a phone call and, once again, clench your buttocks or your thighs making sure you keep your centre of gravity low.

Remember, just let the words flow gently. You are not trying to sell. You are not trying to sound impressive. You are not trying to force anything.

Speaking from a low centre of gravity is what will make the difference.

Try it.

EXERCISE 8

Articulation exercises

Having done your *Humpty Dumpty* tongue exercise, you can continue to 'take your tongue to the gym' with these articulation exercises.

It is important that you do them fairly quietly. You are not trying to strain your throat, you are trying to get your tongue moving. These exercises are not about volume. Start slowly and very clearly. Don't try to make them sound conversational. You are taking your tongue to the gym. Try to hit every sound, every consonant. Almost over-articulate them.

Then, when you have got your tongue around them, you can start to speed up. But beware of speeding up before you can get your tongue around the words. And avoid the temptation to get louder as you get faster. This is a light workout for your throat and a heavy work out for your tongue.

Round the ragged rock
The ragged rascal ran.

Red leather, yellow leather.
Red leather, yellow leather.

Betty bought a bit of butter
But she found the butter bitter,
So she bought a bit of better butter
To make the bitter butter better.

How much wood could a woodchuck chuck,
If a wood-chuck could chuck wood?

Peter Piper picked a peck of pickled peppers.
A peck of pickled peppers Peter Piper picked.
If Peter Piper picked a peck of pickled peppers,
Where's the peck of pickled peppers Peter Piper picked?

I saw Susie sitting in a shoe shine shop.

I scream, you scream, we all scream for ice-cream!

The thirty-three thieves
Thought they thrilled
The throne throughout Thursday.

The World Wide Web

All I want is a proper cup of coffee
made in a proper copper coffee pot.
I may be off my dot, but I want a cup of coffee
in a proper coffee pot.
Tin coffee pots and iron coffee pots,
they're no use to me.
If I can't have a proper cup of coffee
in a proper copper coffee pot,
I'll have a cup of tea.

5

Your Body Language

Obviously we all know how to stand. But when we stand up to speak in public, all of a sudden our bodies seem to behave weirdly and we feel self-conscious. We often don't know what to do with our hands and most parts of our body seem oddly alien to us.

As we know, this is all part of the fight or flight response. We feel under attack (judged) by the audience and all our senses are on edge. We feel exposed. It is not dissimilar to the dream where we find ourselves in public with no clothes on.

If we are trying to make a good impression - both socially and in business - we often smile and hold contact with the other person's eyes as we shake their hand. The difficulty is that we also give off thousands of unconscious signals through our body language that other people will read instantly and instinctively. For example, if we happen to stand in the same way as someone who has treated them badly in the past - perhaps a teacher or a colleague - they might subconsciously feel hostile. And, of course, the reverse is true. If we happen to move like someone they adore, our overtures might be greeted with smiles.

We can never know the history of the other person or the audience, but we can do our best to give out open, clear and non-mixed body language messages.

There have been several studies over the years into how audiences respond. I'm sure you will be familiar with the most often quoted report which suggests that 55% of an audience's judgement is on the visual clues we give out (our body language), 38% on our voice and only 7% on what we are actually saying. In fact these figures were taken from an experiment where the speaker was being deliberately incongruent, so I'm not sure the figures are totally accurate. But there is no doubt that a large part of an audience's judgement of us is visual and vocal.

We tend to believe what we see. If you nod when saying 'No' or shake your head when saying 'Yes', we'll probably believe what your head is doing, rather than the words you've used.

If you say 'This has been a terrible month', we would probably take it on face value. But if you said, 'This has been a terrible month', followed by a wink and a smile, we'll assume you're being ironic and that actually it has been a great month.

Our audience will sense something isn't quite right when we say one thing but look like we're saying another. They may not know what it is but something will be niggling away in their subconscious.

And a smile, of course, needs to fill the whole face. If you say you're happy but your eyes are sad - even though your mouth is smiling - we will believe the eyes.

In the 1960 TV debate between John F. Kennedy and Richard Nixon, both candidates answered well. But on a poll conducted the next day, there were completely different results between TV and radio audiences - between those who had seen and heard and those who had only heard. Listeners on radio were convinced Nixon had won the debate, his arguments were clear. But the larger audience, who watched on TV, were convinced Kennedy had won. He came across as likeable and believable. This was despite the fact that Nixon's arguments were probably clearer.

People believed Kennedy more - they bought into his body language and the signals he gave of. They didn't trust Nixon because of his body language.

Let us learn to send out the right 'open' signals - as if we are saying to our audience, 'Trust me.'

Think about all the non-verbal communication signals you give out - both conscious and unconscious. Think about your body movements and gestures. Are they aggressive or non-threatening? Do you look tired or angry? Calm or nervous?

There are basically five types of body language. I'm sure you will recognise these five types easily:

CLOSED / AGGRESSIVE:
Over firm handshake
'Eye balling' - out staring
Invading personal space - standing too close
Aggressive gesturing or pointing
Legs too wide

CLOSED / DEFENSIVE
Crossed arms or legs
Hunched shoulders
Poor eye contact
Leaning away
Tight throat

CLOSED / NERVOUS
Weak handshake
Avoiding eye contact
Dry throat – swallowing/coughing
Blushing – face/neck/chest
Fidgeting

CLOSED / BORED
Yawning
Shifting weight
Rubbing face
Looking around the room
Drumming fingers

OPEN / INTERESTED
Firm handshake
Good eye contact
Confident stance
Confident, chosen gestures
Showing interest, with a head nod or a slight lean in

In some situations it's hard to be open. We all know that we 'close off' in an elevator to feel safer as our personal space is invaded. We look up or down and cross our arms. This is an obvious case of 'closed' body language. It might be appropriate in an elevator but in most other situations, it will 'close' the other person down. They will not respond to our advances.

Learning to give 'open' signals will 'open' people up to our ideas and advances. Clearly we should be aiming for open and interested body language when we stand to give a talk.

Most of us can recognise the most common 'closed' or 'aggressive' body language signals, but we give off far more subtle signals all the time that we might not be aware of.

You can change your body language to show empathy and to influence someone by, for example, slowing down your movements or taking away any unintended aggressive body language of your own.

You can learn to relax, calm and excite other people purely by the way you hold yourself, the way you move and the way you interact.

Working with a coach can be really helpful - the coach can act as a mirror, feeding back how the world 'sees' you. Or you could watch yourself back on video.

I remember a tennis coach telling me that I didn't take my arm back far enough when hitting the ball.

'I do take it back far enough,' I insisted.

It was only when I actually saw how short my backswing was on video that I knew the coach had been right.

Let's first have a look at how we stand when we give a talk. If we can learn to give off the right body language signals, we not only look confident but feel it too.

How should I stand?

We want to appear calm when we stand to speak. We don't want the audience to be distracted by unnecessary or erratic movements.

Of course, it's hard to stand still when the old fight or flight response rears its ugly head. The brain is saying 'run' and so we feel the urge to move.

If we move on an idea then it will seem logical to the audience but if we move simply because we are too nervous to stand still, then it will be distracting.

If you were acting in a play and your character wanted a drink, you might move to get one. You might also go to get a drink as an excuse to move away from the person you're talking to. A move should always linked to an idea or a thought.

Some speakers hold on to the lectern, with one hand gently on each side to steady them. This stops them moving about and deals with the issue of what to do with their hands but it will lock them into one position and the lectern acts as a barrier between them and the audience.

To stop yourself aimlessly wandering around the stage as you speak, plant your feet firmly on the floor about hip width apart.

If they are too close together you won't be balanced and you risk falling over. If they are too wide apart you could end up looking like John Wayne.

Make sure that your weight is evenly distributed between both feet. This is very important to make you feel centred. Having your weight on one hip will inevitably pull you off centre.

What do I do with my hands?

What do we do with our hands at a dinner party or in the pub? Or when we're playing with our kids? The answer is we don't know. We don't have to think about it - our hands just do what our hands usually do.

But stand up in public and our arms suddenly seem to be twice as long and twice as gangly. Not only that, but our hands seem to belong to someone else.

There are basically five ways to place your hands when you're giving a talk:

1.   Hold your hands behind your back.

Some people like this position because it can help to stop them shaking. You can 'lock' your hands down - but doing this can also tighten your chest and your voice.

This position can look formal and a bit military. It's also very hard to make a gesture if you keep your hands behind your back - let alone turn over your notes.

2.   Cross your arms in front of you.

This position feels remarkably comfortable. I often stand with my arms crossed when watching my kids play sport and I don't feel particularly rude when talking to other parents on the touchline. But it looks more closed than it feels. You can speak with your arms crossed occasionally, perhaps later on in your talk, but never in first few minutes.

We must learn to give out open signals right from the start. And remember that audiences make *blink* judgements of you. If they have never seen you before and they see you with crossed arms, their body language *blink* of you is that you are 'closed'. Not a great start.

3. Stick your hands in your pockets.

The audience's *blink* judgement here is the same as having your hands behind your back. Hands in pockets looks like you're hiding something. Your nerves? Or the truth perhaps? Either way it's a mixed message.

Many people, when feeling a bit nervous, try to look relaxed with their hands in their pockets, as if saying 'Hey, I'm so relaxed, it's just like you've come round for a beer.' But the audience can spot that they are merely trying to 'act' relaxed. A classic mixed message.

Again, as with crossed hands, I am talking about the first few minutes. A bit later on, one hand in a pocket might be fine. But for most situations, certainly with an external audience or with customers, I wouldn't recommend chancing this one in the first few minutes.

4. Hands hanging by your side.

Technically, this is open body language but it often feels a little false and studied. In real life situations, people rarely stand like this.

Many speakers look as if their hands are dangling there like dead weights and often feel the urge to swing them like church bells. It can look a bit odd.

The main reason I wouldn't recommend standing with our hands by our side, is that it leaves our emotional centre wide open. At a subconscious level we feel deeply exposed when our emotional centre is unprotected.

5. Hold your hands lightly together in front of your lower stomach.

This is the stance that most professional presenters prefer. It is good for three reasons.

Firstly, you are protecting (comforting) your emotional centre, and so you will feel less vulnerable in front of an audience.

Secondly, you are free to make gestures, with either one hand or two. When you've finished the gesture, you can simply return the hand or hands to their default position, held lightly together in front of your lower stomach.

And lastly, it looks 'open', while at the same time making you feel comfortable and protected.

Speaking when sitting down

We have learned how to stay centred when standing up, but how can we stay centred when sitting down to speak?

Firstly, never trust the back of a chair. You can end up leaning too far back, especially if you are visiting a client and sitting in an unfamiliar chair. If you lean too far back you will tighten your throat area, as here:

So I recommend sitting forward on your chair. Ideally your feet should be flat on the ground and you should be slightly leaning forward.

In this position, your neck and throat areas are relaxed and your lungs can move freely to give you enough air to speak well.

You will look and feel more 'dynamic' if you sit in this position. You can also rise with excitement if you wanted to.

Your hands should be kept in view whenever possible. Studies have shown that you are more likely to get a job in an interview if you place your hands on the table in front of you, rather than hiding them on your lap under the table.

On a body language level, hiding our hands can be seen as hiding something - our nerves or our true intentions. So sit forward, with your feet firmly on the ground, your back slightly leaning in, your hands on the table in front of you and breathe into your lower stomach.

Know how you are going to stand at the start

If you have decided how you are going to stand before you reach the podium, you will have taken out one of the biggest elements of chance from the start of your talk.

I have enough to think about at the start of a talk without thinking about how I'm going to stand, so I always stand in exactly the same way.

1. I place my feet hip width apart, with my weight evenly distributed to make me look and feel centred.

2. I clench my thighs to lower my centre of gravity, stop any shaking and take any tension away from my throat.

3. I hold my hands lightly together in front of my lower stomach, gently protecting my emotional centre.

4. Then I smile.

That's it. Very simple. Four things. And away you go.

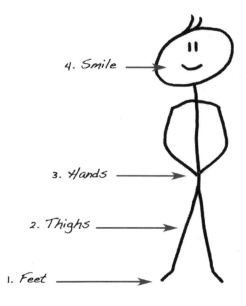

EXERCISE 1

Sitting down

Imagine you are going to present at a board meeting.

Sit right back in a chair with your legs crossed and say:

'Good morning, Ladies and Gentlemen. Thank you for coming.'

Now sit forward, with your bottom near the front of the chair, your feet firmly on the floor, and say again:

'Good morning, Ladies and Gentlemen. Thank you for coming.'

You should notice that your voice is stronger. This is a good position in which to present at a meeting. You should feel centred and will look confident.

There are times, of course, when you might choose a more relaxed stance. Experiment with different ways of sitting and observe how they each make you sound and feel.

Think how your audience might react to you if you spoke from these different positions.

EXERCISE 2

Standing up

Stand up and go through the four point check list for standing that we looked at in this chapter:

Feet. Thighs. Hands. Smile.

So now you should be standing with your feet firmly on the floor and your weight evenly distributed. This will make you look and feel centred. Your hands are held gently together in front of your lower stomach.

Smile and say:

'Good morning, Ladies and Gentlemen. Thank you for coming.'

Now try having your hands hanging by your side and say:

'Good morning, Ladies and Gentlemen. Thank you for coming.'

How does that feel? Your emotional centre is exposed in this position. Try speaking again but with your hands gently back together in front of your lower stomach:

'Good morning, Ladies and Gentlemen. Thank you for coming.'

Your emotional centre is now covered. Do you feel more relaxed and comfortable in this position? Do you feel less exposed?

EXERCISE 3

Hand gestures

Stand with your weight evenly distributed.

Try moving one hand in an open gesture, like an Italian might do, as you say this sentence:

'This is a fantastic idea.'

Hand gestures, of course, can reinforce our message.

Try saying it again, but this time gesturing with both hands, as if your are suggesting an amazing idea:

'This is an absolutely incredible idea.'

When you have finished speaking, bring your hands together again in front of your lower stomach, almost as if a magnet was pulling them back.

Now try saying it again but this time only move your hands from your wrists:

'This is an absolutely incredible idea.'

This will feel odd. Did it change the sound of your voice? Perhaps it sounded tighter and more restricted?

Try saying it again both ways, with open relaxed gestures using your whole arms and then with small tight gestures that start from your wrists. By experimenting in this way you can learn which gestures work best for you.

Always return your hands to their neutral position in front of your lower stomach. If you get used to having your hands here, you will never have to think about what to do with your hands again when speaking in public.

6

Your Structure

Before you start to structure your speech, you need to ask yourself three essential questions:

Why are you giving this talk?

Why should the audience care?

What are you really saying?

Only when you have answered these three questions can you start to work on your structure.

1. Why are you giving this talk?

Are you giving this talk to inform, sell, persuade, motivate, anger, harmonise, neutralize or create controversy?

We must always have a reason for giving a talk.

What do you want from it?

What do you want the audience to do as result of your giving it?

Most talks fall into two basic categories. To sell or to motivate.

To sell

If you are giving a talk to sell, then you will be either selling a product or selling an idea.

We can all spot sales pitches for products or sales pitches for support - as in a politician asking for your vote.

Then there are sales pitches asking for your time - as in a local charity asking you to give your time to help a community project.

When we are selling something as a speaker, we will always want something from our audience - either their money, their support or their time.

To motivate

You might be giving a talk to motivate your sales team.

Or you might be persuading an audience to think differently about something. Motivational talks are about changing beliefs and behaviors.

We might think a political campaigner urging their audience to think differently is a motivational talk, but it could actually be a sales talk in disguise - asking them to buy into their ideas and then to vote for them.

You might be giving a talk about a recent holiday and suggesting that your audience might like to go there too. You are offering them a suggestion, so this would be a motivational talk - unless, of course, you happen to be a travel agent.

If you're speaking at a wedding, you might want to move the audience emotionally. You might want to make them laugh or tell them how you feel.

If you were giving a talk at the local historical society about a local landmark, you might want to engage their interest in the landmark and then ask them to tell others about it. But it would become a sales talk if we were ultimately trying to get people to buy tickets to visit it or to sponsor its upkeep.

A motivational speech is trying to inspire, encourage or move emotionally.

So once you know whether you are trying to sell or to motivate, what do you want your audience to do after your talk?

Buy your product?
Agree with your proposal?
Support you?
Spread the word?
Behave differently?
Think differently?
Feel differently?
Feel connected?
Be inspired to change a belief or an action?

If you know why you are giving this talk, you can make sure that you construct it in the best way so that the audience will want to *buy* from you, or are *motivated* by you.

It is when a speaker has forgotten to ask this first question that a talk might seem boring to the audience. 'That was a complete waste of time. What was all that about? Why did I bother to come along today?'

But if we are really clear why we are giving the talk, then our audience will be really clear why they should care.

People sometimes say that they're not really giving a talk, they're *just* giving their team an update. The word 'just' underpins how they really feel about it. If the speaker is already bored by it, then so will the audience be.

We should never *just* give information.

Actor Ralph Richardson said, 'Acting is merely the art of keeping a large group of people from coughing.' We keep them from coughing when giving a speech too, by keeping them interested. And we do that by telling them what to feel about what we are saying. If we are merely giving them information, they probably won't care.

A client once said to me that it was OK for me to be enthusiastic when I speak as communication is an interesting topic, but he sold aluminium chairs and he thought the audience would find that aluminium was boring.

'Hang on,' I said to the group. 'Does anyone here know the exact temperature that aluminium is heated to so that it will bend to form a perfect curve but not crack?' No one did but they were all intrigued to know the exact temperature. So I said, 'No, nor do I, but I've got your attention.' Aluminium is no more or less boring than anything else. As always, it is the speaker's attitude to a subject that matters. If they care, the audience will care.

If we are giving an update on the latest sales figures we must interpret them. Are they good or bad? Interesting or expected? Worrying or exciting? It is in our interpretation that a speech or talk becomes meaningful. Our interpretation of the facts keeps an audience's attention alive.

So now that we know why you are giving your talk, we can go on to answer the second important question.

2. Why should the audience care?

In the 1960's a company selling lawn seed ran this advertising campaign:

THE BEST LAWN SEED IN THE WORLD.

Their sales didn't go up when the commercial was running. Something was wrong. They soon realised that their audience didn't want a great lawn seed. What the audience wanted was a great lawn. So they changed their strapline to:

FOR THE BEST LAWNS IN THE WORLD.

Their sales shot up.

Always remember what's in it for the audience.

Are we going to help them make more money? Teach them something new? Make their lives easier? Or change their lives altogether?

Telling them what's in it for them will grab their attention right at the start.

Before you structure or deliver your talk, think about your audience.

What is your relationship with them? Are they your peers, superiors or your team? Are they your customers or in your supply chain?

How much credibility do you have with them? What other factors may influence how they see you? Why should they care about what you are saying?

I remember working on a corporate training film for car salesmen many years ago. It was a video about matching the emotional levels of excitement between the customer and the sales person.

When we are thinking of buying a new car we are excited as we enter the showroom for a test drive. But the moment we sign the deal, we worry whether we've done the right thing and we hit our lowest emotional point.

And, of course, that's exactly when the dealer hits their highest emotional point - they know they've just got themselves a deal and earned their commission.

It's only a few days later, when we arrive to pick up our brand new car, that we hit our emotional high point. And that's exactly when the dealer hits their lowest point - they're more interested in other customers in the showroom than in showing us round a car they've already sold.

So the film was teaching sales teams to remember to put themselves in the place of their customers every step of the way.

The same is true of giving a speech. We must always try to understand what our audience might be thinking. We could be being very enthusiastic, just when the audience still need persuading. We don't want our enthusiasm to fall on deaf ears.

Putting ourselves in the place of the audience is Zone Two behaviour. It helps build empathy and will encourage them to join us in their Zone Two.

But understanding what our audience might be thinking isn't enough. We must tell them that we understand their point of view. We must show them in the choice of the words we use and the way we say them.

However, remember that we can only make an informed 'guess' about how they might be feeling.

It's generally safer to preface our guesses with 'You might be worried about ...' or 'Some people might feel ...'

'Sell the sizzle not the sausage.'

This famous phrase, used in the advertising industry in the 1960s, meant we should sell the benefit of the product or an idea and not just the product or idea itself.

Too many talks tell the audience how brilliant the speaker is or how brilliant their ideas are, but not always what's in it for the audience.

The next time we give a talk, remember to tell the audience what's in it for them.

3. What are you really saying?

You're probably familiar with Mind Maps. I find them really helpful in the construction of a talk. I use them to tell stories logically and to keep the audience on message from start to finish.

Mind Maps have a series of circles stemming from one central circle outlining key words in an organic, tree-like structure.

In the centre circle you would write your key message, your central idea, in just a few words.

Let's take a simple example - a corporate talk about which suppliers to use. We must be really specific here. It's very tempting to put SUPPLIERS as our central idea. But that would be too general.

Here are four suggestions of a more specific key message:

We should use these suppliers.
We should not use these suppliers.
We should never have used these suppliers.
We should not use any suppliers.

So if we were to give this talk, we would start with a large sheet of paper and draw a small circle in the middle. In it we would write our key message. Let's use the first suggestion - We should 'use these suppliers':

That's your starting point. Your key message. It's unambiguous and makes the point clearly and upfront.

If we start with our key message, we will 'hold' our audience.

It's so much better than speaking generally about suppliers and then suggesting why we should use these particular ones after ten minutes of waffle.

From here we will start to build our mind map 'tree', adding in other branches of our story, while making sure that the key message stays the key message.

In the early days of Hollywood, if you had an idea for a film, you'd hope to catch the film producer and pitch your story right there and then. An elevator was a great place to trap a producer. But you only had the time it took from the ground floor to the executive floor in which to pitch it, so this became known as the 'elevator pitch'. And it's a good idea to have an 'elevator pitch' for every talk you give.

I hear talks almost every day and often by the end I'm not exactly sure why I've been given that information. I can remember much of what has been said but not always the elevator pitch, the central theme, the main idea.

We must always know what our key message is. We must always know what we are really saying.

Leonora, the six year old daughter of a friend of mine, was watching politicians on TV. She said, 'I think they are speaking a different language.' I asked her, 'Is that because you don't understand what they are saying?' 'No,' she replied, 'they don't sound as if they understand what they are saying.'

We don't want Leonora ever to say that about us.

But before we start thinking about structuring your talk, let's have a quick look at what the ancient Greeks had to say about structure, over 2000 years ago.

Rhetoric

In his book *Rhetoric,* Aristotle suggested that to persuade, influence or move an audience, we must follow this basic structure:

Ethos, Logos and *Pathos.* (And no, they're not Greek islands as a recent client suggested.)

Ethos is about building empathy and rapport, gaining the audience's trust in us as someone they can believe in.

Logos is about persuading an audience that our argument makes sense. It's not simply that our idea makes logical sense, we have to actually persuade them that it make sense.

And finally, *Pathos.* This is where we should engage the audience on an emotional level. We must inspire and motivate them.

But if we try to move our audience emotionally (*Pathos*) before we have either established rapport (*Ethos*) or persuaded them that our argument makes sense (*Logos*), then we may not win them over.

Ethos, Logos and *Pathos.* In that order.

Trust. Prove. Motivate.

One of the best examples of *Ethos* is Mark Antony's funeral oration in Shakespeare's *Julius Caesar:*

'Friends, Romans, Countrymen, lend me your ears.'

He establishes rapport with his audience right away, suggesting he is one of them, a 'friend' and a fellow 'Roman'. His use of 'Countrymen' suggests his love of his whole country. So he has established an immediate trust and bond.

Using my furniture shop example from Chapter 2, a salesman could use these three steps to sell a chair:

Ethos: establishing trust -'Buy this chair because, believe me, I know a lot about chairs.'

Logos: persuasion and reasoned argument - 'Your last chair broke after two weeks. This one is much stronger.'

Pathos: appealing to their emotions - 'This is a green chair. It is environmentally friendly.'

Rhetorica ad Herennium

300 years after Aristotle came *Rhetorica ad Herennium* (originally attributed to the Roman philosopher, Cicero).

This book divides speeches into six parts:

1. *Exordium*: getting the audience's attention and proving that you have the knowledge to speak.

2. *Narratio*: outlining your argument.

3. *Divisio*: showing where you and your opponents agree.

4. *Confirmatio*: supporting your own case.

5. *Refutatio*: smash your opponent's argument to pieces.

6. *Conclusio*: The grand finale including lots of pathos.

So bearing all that in mind, now let's look at how best to structure your talk.

How should you start?

Most talks start something like this:

'Hello, my name is Robin. I'd like to talk to you for about 20 or 25 minutes, if that's ok. Then perhaps we'll have some questions. So if we are all ready, I'll start.'

It's predictable, not particularly interesting and pretty boring. We can do without generalised 'waffle', especially at the start of a talk.

And we want to avoid an opening 'Terminal Five' moment.

When Heathrow's brand new Terminal Five first opened in 2008, there was chaos in the luggage-handling area. Despite the fact that the Terminal now runs brilliantly, people still remember that dreadful start.

So let's not start with a 'Terminal Five' moment. Instead, let's start really well.

Here are some of the best ways to grab our audience's attention right from the word go.

The Headline Method

The conductor Thomas Beecham said there are two golden rules for an orchestra: 'Start together and finish together; the public doesn't give a damn what happens in between.'

So first, let's start really well and grab the audience's attention.

I often suggest the Headline method of starting. It can make even the novice appear brilliant. When you read a newspaper story, you are first grabbed by the headline. This is what makes you want to read on. Then we are introduced to the central theme - the key message in the centre of the Mind Map. The Headline has pulled you in and now you want to read on. It's exactly the same with a speech.

After our Headline start, we have the meat in the middle of the 'story sandwich.'

And then, at the end, we want to finish really well too. In the Headline method we finish as we began, by repeating the opening phrase.

However tempting it is to get into detail straight away or even end on the detail, remember no-one ever read a book to get to the middle. The middle is the middle, but the start and the finish are special.

Audiences will remember the first and last thing we say.

The Headline method works every time and is particularly useful when giving impromptu talks.

Here's a scenario: It's my brother's birthday and someone asks me to say a few words. I don't have time to write a speech but if I use the Headline method, the audience will probably think that I have planned it and I will feel great because I started well and finished well.

All I have to do is to come up with a Headline. It doesn't have to be earth-shatteringly brilliant, but it does have to sum up what the talk is about.

I'll opt for, 'My brother is the best brother in the world.'

Then I will have to make up the rest of the speech on the spot - the middle section will inevitably have to be more free form and spontaneous.

When I've finished, or can't think of anything else to say, I simply repeat the Headline and finish confidently. In this case, I might end with, 'So that's why my brother is the best brother in the world. Thank you very much.'

A client had to speak at his Aunt's funeral recently and he asked me if I had any ideas as to how to approach his eulogy. I asked him to describe his Aunt. 'Oh, that's easy,' he said. 'She was very funny.'

I suggested that he had almost written his speech, and that he start by putting the words, 'My Aunt was a very funny lady', in the centre of his Mind Map.

All he had to do now was think of a couple of stories about why his Aunt was funny, and then at the end repeat his Headline.

He ended his eulogy with, 'So when you think of my Aunt, think of her as a very funny lady.'

You can see how well this can work in many different situations.

Start well and finish well.

Five ways to start using the Headline Method

Let's look at several ways we can grab an audience's attention using the Headline method: The Hook, the Tease, the Question, the Shock and the Three Way opening.

In this example, let's suppose our talk is about encouraging the audience to invest their money. The words in the centre of our Mind Map are 'I can double your money.'

The Hook:

'I'm going to show you how you can double your money in the next five minutes.'

The Tease:

'I'm going to show you how you can double your money in the next five minutes ... but first I'd like to tell you something else ...'

The Question:

'Who here would like to double your money in the next five minutes?'

The Shock:

'If we don't double our money in the next five minutes, we're toast.'

The Three Way opening:

'I *could* tell you about the current state of the world economy; I *could* tell you about how ill prepared most of us are in our retirement planning; but *instead* I think I'll start by telling you how you can double your money in the next five minutes.'

Let's have a look at some other ways of starting a talk.

The dramatic start

I once saw a CEO abseiling into his company conference from the ceiling, accompanied by pyrotechnics and the 'Mission Impossible' theme tune.

Watch some of the most memorable TED talks on YouTube and you can see some dramatic, off-the-wall starts.

Jamie Oliver dumped a wheelbarrow of sugar on stage to demonstrate how much sugar there is in milk in the USA.

Jill Bolte Taylor carried on a real human brain as a prop.

Comedian and TV presenter Bruce Forsyth once brought a camera on stage and asked the audience to pose for a picture. After the flash bulb went off he said, 'It's for my mother - she doesn't believe I have a proper job.'

All these are ways of grabbing the audience's attention. They are unexpected.

Try bringing on a tiny dictionary and looking up a very long word.

Or take out your mobile phone and call the House of Commons.

Or speak the lyrics of a well known song. In French.

You can also be dramatic when pitching.

Imagine you were asking for your boss's approval to green light a project. You could say, 'Imagine you have two large buttons on the desk in front of you. One says YES, one says NO. In a few moments I'm going to ask you to push one of those buttons.'

Then after your pitch, you can ask directly which button they will press. This is not as much of a gamble as it might seem. They will have to make a Yes/No decision at some stage anyway. This might encourage them to make a quicker decision than they might otherwise have done.

If you feel passionately about something, try the dramatic start. Whatever is appropriate. Whatever works.

Start by posing a problem

You can start a talk by posing a problem and then go on to solve it.

For example:

'For several years now, we've become aware that many of our customers are thinking about leaving us. They haven't actually left yet but they will unless we do something. And fast. I have an idea that might help …'

Start by using a Quotation

To quote or not to quote? A quotation from a well-known person can work well. It can add credibility to your argument if it confirms your key message. But I would steer away from using a quote from someone they have never heard of.

I generally don't like speeches that start with, 'As X once said …' I tend to sit in the audience thinking, 'Yes, but what do *you* say?!'

Picture a scene

The idea here is to create a scene that the audience can easily visualize. 'Imagine yourself in the Bahamas, lying on a warm, tranquil beach, not a cloud in the sky ...'

This can work well, because it jumps straight into the story, which I love. Also audiences generally find it easier to remember visual images.

But this doesn't work every time. I remember the violinist Sir Yehudi Menuhin giving a talk at my school when I was nine years old. He started with the exciting words, 'I'm going to take you on a journey ...'

I imagined the coach outside ready to take us away for the day and got very excited. But sadly he continued, '... Of course, I mean a *musical* journey.'

My heart sank. Perhaps his start might have worked better with adults.

Anecdote

A good anecdote can work well. A good personal anecdote can work even better.

But only if it's relevant. Anecdotes that are shoe-horned into a speech for no reason will stand out a mile.

Keep your eyes and ears open for interesting anecdotes and stories. Write them in a notebook.

I have a file on my computer desktop labelled *ONE DAY*. I put all sort of things in there, stories, anecdotes and quotes, because I never know, one day I may need them ...

Topical start

You could start by referring to a topical item. This can make you look relaxed enough to have adapted your talk on the day, making you appear spontaneous.

Read a newspaper or listen to the radio on your way to the venue for appropriate topical ideas.

Refer to the locality

Linking your start to the locality of the venue can build empathy with your audience. Pop stars tend to get a huge cheer as they say 'Hello, London!' or wherever into the microphone at the start of a concert.

I'm not suggesting that screaming 'Hello, Wolverhampton!' when giving a sales talk to your local suppliers is necessarily going to get a cheer from your audience, but a reference to their home football team might do the trick.

Wrong-footing the audience

One of my favourite openings to a speech was by Pam Ayres, the wonderful Oxfordshire poet.

She said that when she was a young girl, her sister was given a doll. She had never been given a doll - which really upset her. So one day when her sister was out, she went into her sister's room and picked up the doll. She tore off both of its arms, then both its legs. And when her sister found the doll in pieces, her sister cried. As Pam looked out at the audience she said, 'And when I saw my sister cry, I laughed … Now, I'm only telling you this in case any of you were thinking of upsetting me tonight by heckling.'

Brilliant.

Another good opening I heard was, 'In the 17th and 18th century, men shaved their heads and wore large ostentatious wigs. And when they fought duels, as they often did, they would try to flick their opponent's wig with the point of their sword and literally pull the wool over their eyes. Now I don't want to pull the wool over your eyes tonight but I would like to tell you about ...'

Grabbing the audience's attention and then wrong-footing them can work well.

The comparison start

You could try starting with a quirky fact. For example:

'I wonder how much it would cost to buy a soap bubble, if there was only one in the world? And what, if after you'd bought it, it popped? Some things are far too valuable to put a price on - like the happiness of your child.'

'IKEA printed 208 million catalogues last year. We haven't printed quite that many here at The Corner Shop but we have given away over five hundred brochures in our first week.'

'Luxembourg is roughly the size of Oxfordshire. Which, as it happens, is about the same size as our new sales area.'

Start in the middle of a story

'So there I was wearing my bright blue jumper. It was my seventh birthday and as I looked up, a man handed me a large gold-wrapped parcel and said, 'Happy birthday, son.' That was the first time I met Elvis Presley.'

We could have started with, 'I first met Elvis Presley when I was seven.' It might have worked but it doesn't set up the excitement of a seventh birthday, and missed the added detail of the bright blue jumper. Telling us that the man was Elvis at the end of the sentence has more impact.

Starting a talk with 'So there I was ...' immediately transports an audience into the story. And if audiences are going to remember the first thing we say, then let us make it really count.

Of course, most of us had never met Elvis Presley, let alone were given a large gold-wrapped parcel by him at our seventh birthday party, but we all have stories to tell. Here is an example of a more everyday situation, but by its construction it would still draw us in.

'The rain was pounding down on the roof of the car as the engine cut out. I'd hoped to be home by midnight but clearly that wasn't going to happen now. After calling the AA, I switched on the car radio, when I heard this advertisement ...'

A talk starting like that would grab our attention right from the word go. We have no idea where the talk is going but that doesn't matter. By starting so confidently, we relax and assume the speaker knows where he or she is going.

So that's got us started. Now let's have a look at our content.

The Fairy Tale Template:

Here's a very simple five part template to hang a story on.

1. Once upon a time there was a …
2. They used to do this …
3. Then one day something changed …
4. So they …
5. And as a result they …

We can adapt the language, of course, depending on the situation. But in a business meeting it might sound something like this:

(1) Many years ago, Mrs X founded this Company.
(2) She had a vision and built up the business over ten years.
(3) Last year she was approached to sell the company.
(4) So she thought about it carefully.
(5) But eventually she decided not to sell. And I'm happy to say that we are still an independent company and growing fast.

At the end of this chapter there is an exercise where you can try this template out for yourself.

Tell stories.

We liked them as children and we like them as adults.

Tell stories

'We do not remember days; we remember moments.'
(Cesare Pavese)

It's often surprising what a major part very small moments play in our lives. I must have been to countless school concerts and plays but there is one moment I can remember above all: the look on my stepson's face the moment he won the school poetry competition at the age of 12. Priceless and unforgettable.

And in the world of work, we are unlikely to remember an entire seminar, but we will probably remember all the stories.

If we want to make it really easy for an audience to remember our message, tell stories.

We can tell stories about ourselves. This helps create empathy. But they must be used at the right time and for the right reasons. Stories purely chosen to make us look good is Zone Three behaviour. And random or irrelevant stories can be distracting and unhelpful.

We could use a parable (a short story about somebody or something else that mirrors what might be happening here). A parable can be a good way to deliver uncomfortable information, without making an audience feel told off.

If you feel that you're not that great at writing stories, we can always adapt other people's stories.

And remember, if you steal directly from one person, it's called plagiarism; but if you steal from loads of people its called research.

Keep it simple:

'If you can't explain it to a six year old, you don't understand it yourself.' (Albert Einstein)

Einstein also said that his greatest idea was to boil an egg in his soup rather than in water, thus saving both on energy and the washing up.

He was keen on simplicity. It's not simple. In fact, it's hard to achieve.

I once sat at dinner next to a top brain surgeon. He explained brain surgery to me in simple terms. And you know what? I got it. I understood it. Of course, I couldn't perform brain surgery as a result of his five minute explanation, but he had given me the basic understanding that I'd asked for. And no more. He didn't over complicate it or baffle me with medical science, so I kept up and didn't get lost.

He obviously knew more than I did but he wasn't at all condescending. He didn't make me feel stupid for not knowing precisely how brain surgery worked. There is another benefit to simplifying like this. By not trying to big himself up, he had encouraged me into my Zone Two. I was now much more likely to listen to him. His Zone Two behavior, being open and welcoming, had encouraged me into my Zone Two.

We can have loads of detail in our talk or presentation but we must also have clarity and simplicity within that detail.

We often say that something was 'deceptively simple', implying that a lot of hard work had been done to cut out any extraneous complications so that the story could be told with simple clarity.

Mark Twain said it took him more than 3 weeks to prepare a good impromptu speech.

We can start by trying not to use unnecessarily complicated words. I know we all like to look clever when we stand up there, but how often do we hear a speaker deliver a 'written' speech?

A written speech is not the same as a spoken speech.

When we write sentences we often use sub-clauses because we've had time to construct a complex thought. But only the truly great minds of playwrights and thinkers can think in sub-clauses on the spur of the moment.

When we lesser mortals deliver convoluted sentences, which we have pre-thought out, they will usually sound unnatural and stilted when we deliver them.

Also pre-written sentences are often longer than spoken ones, and unless we are very clever we tend to speak in shorter 'sound bites'. Politicians regularly speak in sound bites to reinforce their message because they can be edited and replayed quickly.

I once asked a group to describe their favourite holiday. One of the men stood up and said, 'There was a magnificent vista from my balcony bay window.'

That is brochure-speak. He wouldn't have used those words to his friends in the pub. He might have said, 'The view from the balcony was incredible.'

By choosing everyday words, your message will be clearer. For example, say:

use instead of *utilize*,
so instead of *consequently*,
now instead of *at the present time*.

138

We're all aware how ridiculous and pompous corporate jargon can sound. It is non-inclusive to those who don't know a buzzword, phrase or acronym. So de-jargon whenever possible.

Generally, we want our talks to feel like a conversation. We want the audience to feel they are going on a journey of discovery, just as we are.

When standing up in public to speak, the last thing we want to appear is stupid, which is why we often try hard to appear clever. But this can make us choose formal and unnecessarily complicated words that we wouldn't normally use.

And as we speak those formal words, we begin to feel less like ourselves and the less simple our message becomes.

We slowly slip out of Zone Two and we start to lose our confidence and our audience.

'Simplicity is the ultimate sophistication.' (Leonardo da Vinci)

Physicists look to Nature because Nature always choses the simplest route, the one that requires the minimum amount of effort.

Let's have a look at geodistic domes - stick with me on this one. People have been building domes for centuries. But older historic domes needed large supporting walls to keep the entire structure from crashing to the ground.

Geodesic domes are different, they are made up of a series of triangles. Triangles are strong because they have fixed angles, so if you put pressure on one edge, then the force is spread evenly to the other two sides. It's the cascading distribution of pressure that makes geodesic domes so strong, much like the shell of an egg.

There we have it. Nature loves simplicity. In its simplicity lies its strength.

So let our talk have one central theme made up of lots of small, perfectly formed triangles to give it the simplicity, clarity and strength it needs to motivate or to sell our ideas to our audience.

Keep it logical

Once you have a key message, keep your story completely logical, every step of the way. Audiences will follow our story only if the structure makes sense.

Have you ever watched a film and thought, 'The leading character wouldn't have done that?' What might have happened is that a small but vital scene had been taken out during the editing process. The producers, being so close to the story, had forgotten that the deleted scene explained the character's later behaviour. It's exactly the same in a speech. If we miss out even one small step, our argument will jump and the audience will lose their way.

So, having decided on your key message in your Mind Map, draw a series of circles coming off your central circle to progress the story. In this example, the first circle could be about price, the next about quality and another about reliability, etc. This way you keep on track but always starting from the central theme, your key message.

It should ideally read like a road map.

If I said to an audience, 'As a company we have come to a metaphorical T junction. We now have two choices. Left or right. For various business reasons, I think we should go right. Having turned right, we now go along that road, and find we now have another two choices. We can go over the bridge or through the under-pass. I think we should go over the bridge. Having done that, we now face a roundabout with four exits and so we now have four more choices. I think, for various business reasons, we should take the second exit.'

That is a logical journey, explaining the business strategy through the metaphor of a road map. We can follow it easily.

But if I gave the same information in a different order, in an illogical way, then an audience is likely to get lost.

If it's too hard to follow, they start to wander off in their minds. They will start to think about the email they should have sent, the phone call they must make, picking the kids up from school or even when the next coffee break is.

So if instead I had said, 'As a company we have some big choices to make. We could go over the bridge, take the second exit, turn right, take the fourth exit or turn left,' the audience would be completely lost.

But keep our story logical and we stand a good chance of holding the audience's attention.

Be brief

'Be interesting, be enthusiastic ... and don't talk too much.'
(Norman Peale)

We've all heard speakers who say they're going to speak for twenty minutes, and then after about an hour and a half they finally reach their second point.

I was once lucky enough to hear one of Bill Clinton's speechwriters give an after dinner speech. As he was being introduced we were told that he would speak about how to construct the perfect speech.

He stood up, and with a twinkle in his eye, said very slowly,

'Be brief. Be funny. Repeat.
Be brief. Be funny. Repeat.'

Then he sat down and took a sip of wine as if his speech was over.

After enjoying a huge laugh from the audience, he stood up again and said, 'That's it. Really. Be brief. Be funny. Repeat. I'm being paid handsomely to give this talk this evening so I feel I can't leave it there, but that's essentially it. Be brief. Be funny. Repeat.'

Being brief, of course, is not simply saying less. It is saying everything we need to say, but as succinctly as possible.

We have all sat in overlong lectures, where the speaker could have said what they wanted to say in half the time. We squirm in our seats waiting for the next break.

Let that not be us next time.

Keeping to time

I was once speaking at a conference and due to speak at midday for a one hour slot taking us all into lunch. But the other three speakers all overran by ten minutes each, so I only had half an hour (including Question and Answer time). I couldn't run late as the caterers were all set to serve lunch at one o'clock sharp. So I had to quickly adapt what I was going to say.

Luckily I had used a Mind Map when preparing my talk, which meant that I could simply cut out two of my planned strands. The talk still made perfect sense (I hope).

The organizers were very apologetic but I told them not to worry as several people in the audience, upset that they had only heard half my talk, booked me to give my full length talk at their own upcoming conferences.

If I'm asked to speak for 45 minutes, I usually aim for 40. We don't want to bore our audiences, upset the other speakers or anger the caterers.

Once you are happy with your structure, try saying your speech out loud in the privacy of your office or your home.

Reading it silently to yourself in your head or mumbling the words quietly will not give you an accurate timing.

There are two other advantages to speaking your talk out loud.

Firstly, it will highlight any difficult words or phrases that you stumble over. Try saying those 'difficult' phrases again and if you still stumble, change the words or the structure of the sentence.

And secondly, by speaking it out loud, you will activate the motor memory of the mouth which will help you remember your talk when you actually give it.

And on the Big Day really try to keep to this timing.

If you are using slides, the Presenter View has a clock that can help you keep to time. It can tell you how long you have been speaking for - as long as you remember to start it as you set off. Most people intend to do this but in the heat of the moment of starting the talk they often forget and are left with a clock showing 00.00 which is not very helpful.

Alternatively you can set a timer, but make sure you turn it off before it actually bleeps. Nothing looks worse than you being interrupted by your own clock.

Wear a watch, have a clock in your line of sight or ask a friend to wave at you from the back when you have five minutes left.

I simply readjust my analogue watch to midday before I am introduced. And then during the talk, with a quick glance, I can easily tell how long I've spoken for.

Use the right words

'Don't tell me the moon is shining; show me the glint of light on broken glass.' (Anton Chekov)

We don't have to be great writers or wordsmiths to create beautiful sentences. But we should choose our words carefully. They can really help us.

We should think about our choice of words, particularly when having to give bad news. An audience can feel told off very easily by the wrong choice of words.

I remember watching a CEO tell their team that he had discovered an employee had attempted to steal part of the Company's database. Their complex security systems had alerted him to what was happening. His speech went something like this:

'I have some bad news. A colleague of yours has been stealing company information. He has now been fired. As will any of you who have the same idea. Rest assured, our security systems will catch you.'

Yet, the people he was speaking to had done nothing wrong. They were loyal employees who now felt they were under suspicion.

A better choice of words might have been:

'I have some very sad news. You might have heard that a member of staff has been caught attempting to steal the company's database. Our security systems spotted his plans. Rest assured that this has not put the Company, or any of your jobs, into jeopardy. I would like to thank you all for your continued loyalty and hard work.'

I recently visited Blickling Hall, a National Trust property in East Anglia, and noticed a sign on an antique wooden table. It read: 'Too fragile to touch.'

How much better that was than the usual uppercase shout, 'DO NOT TOUCH'. It was better because it really made me want to take care of that fragile table.

The singer Morrissey, of The Smiths, said he always used words that had 'soft edges'. He would have like those words, 'Too fragile to touch.'

Try using words that are 'good on the ear'. Words that we can remember.

The poet e.e. cummings said, 'the world is mud-liscious and puddle-wonderful'. These sorts of phrases make us sit up and listen. They are memorable.

When playwright Tom Stoppard was asked to describe his play *Rosencrantz and Guildenstern Are Dead*, he said it was 'a comedy with a capital K'. I would remember that if I heard that in a talk.

And when speaking about the difference between poetry and prose, he said that, 'Poetry is language on point.' Let us try to use language 'on point' too.

Shakespeare used the rhythm of the human heartbeat, known as iambic pentameter. Five heartbeats per line, as in De Dum De Dum De Dum De Dum De Dum.

Here's a famous example, the last two lines of his sonnet, *'Shall I compare thee to a summer's day?'*:

'So long as men can breathe, or eyes can see,
So long lives this, and this gives life to thee.'

Each line has five heartbeats:

'So **long** as **men** can **breathe**, or **eyes** can **see**,
So **long** lives **this**, and **this** gives **life** to **thee**.'

And this line from *HENRY V*:

'Now all the youth of England are on fire.'

Again, five heartbeats:

'Now **all** the **youth** of **Eng**land **are** on **fire**.'

It has a natural human rhythm and energy.

Here's an example of how we could use it in a business scenario. Imagine a sales manager talking to his team about their customers.

'They buy when they believe we tell the truth.'

Saying this line using the five heartbeat rhythm helps reinforce the message.

'They **buy** when **they** bel-**ieve** we **tell** the **truth**.'

Try it. It works.

Use a simile

Similes can help us understand a difficult concept.

We could say, 'The area of land needed to build our new factory is 10,800 square meters.' Or we could say, 'The area of land needed to build our new factory is roughly the size of a football pitch.' We can all picture a football pitch but we have no idea what 10,800 square meters either looks or feels like.

Winston Churchill

British Prime Minister Winston Churchill learned from the *Rhetoric* of the ancient Greeks and Romans.

One of his favourite *Rhetoric* devices was the use of *Anaphora* (repeating words or phrases at the beginning of a sentence) - as in this well-known example from the Bible:

'A time to be born, a time to die;
A time to plant, a time to reap.'

The original typed script of Churchill's *'We must arm'* speech in 1938, looked like this:

'We must arm.
If through an earnest desire for peace,
we have placed ourselves at a disadvantage,
we must make up for it by redoubled exertions.'

But in the version he actually spoke from, he had added two more sentences, in his own handwriting, to help punctuate and build the *Anaphora* rhythm. He also uses a *Tricolon* - building a phrase in three sections - which works brilliantly:

'We must arm.
Britain must arm.
America must arm.
If through an earnest desire for peace,
we have placed ourselves at a disadvantage,
we must make up for it by redoubled exertions.'

The ancient Greeks and Romans had whole dictionaries dedicated to the structure of phrases, sentences and entire speeches. (Notice my use of the *Tricolon* there?)

Here are a few examples of *Rhetoric* that you might like to try:

Rising Tricolon - three phrases which rise in length and/or importance, as in 'I came, I saw, I conquered.'

Isocolon - balances clauses of the same length and has a good, balanced rhythm, as in 'The more the water came in the boat, the faster I pulled on the oars.'

Captatio Benevolentiae - an appeal to the audience's goodwill by self-conscious humility: 'I may be Prime Minister, but I'm really a grocer's daughter ... '

Praeterito - pretending that you're not going to talk about something but then you go on and talk about it anyway. A favourite of politicians through the ages: 'I'm not going to talk about the mess you've made of the economy. I'm not going to talk about your appalling record on unemployment. I'm going to talk about the biggest mistake that you have made so far, the woeful lack of investment in infrastructure.'

Imagine a TV commercial in the style of *Praeterito*. A female presenter puts a finger to her lips, 'Shh, I know it's not polite to advertise, so I won't tell you about the Diamond Shop Sale. I know I mustn't talk about that. It's a great shame as they have some amazing deals on right now.'

Repetition - used throughout the ages, works brilliantly. It helps us remember a message by reinforcing it.

Rhyme - a form of repetition and can work in the same way.

Alliteration - the repetition of a particular sound, for example: 'dull, dark dock'. It also helps re-enforce the message.

Humour

To be funny or not to be funny?

Humour doesn't always travel well. And as with anecdotes, make sure that a joke is relevant and that it adds something to your story. To get a laugh from an audience, the joke assumes a degree of shared knowledge.

Of course, some people are better at telling jokes than others.

I had a client who had to give a Best Man speech at a wedding. He was panicking and said, 'I'm the Best Man, I have to be funny.'

I assured him that nowhere in the manual does it say the Best Man has to be funny. In fact, if you are not very good at telling jokes, you almost certainly won't be funny. Best not to try.

So instead, I asked him to tell me about his friend Paul who was getting married. 'Oh, that's easy,' he said, 'he's the kindest man on the planet.'

So I suggested he start his speech with that. 'Paul is the kindest man on the planet, and I'm going to tell you why.'

And then he told a few stories about why Paul was the man he was. These included a couple of amusing incidents. It gave the speech some gentle humour and the audience loved it, because it was from the heart. And that's not a bad thing to have at a wedding after all - probably more appropriate than delivering a few unrelated jokes downloaded off the internet.

Try not to repeat the same word too often

You can say your product is 'amazing' once or even twice, but say it seventeen times and amazingly 'amazing' loses its value.

Say the word 'interesting' seventeen times and it ceases to be the slightest bit interesting.

And it would soon become annoying to an audience if you started every sentence with 'OK'.

How to end your talk

'A speech is like a love affair - any fool can start it, but to end it requires considerable skill.' (Lord Mancroft)

We must finish as well as we started.

I often say to clients, if you start and finish really well then it's not a disaster if you're not totally perfect somewhere in the middle. Knowing this can take away some of the performance pressure. Remember that a strong start and finish can work wonders.

When we come to look at the delivery of your talk, in the next chapter, we'll see how important it is to know the first thing you're going to say.

And having the safety net of repeating that Headline at the end will really help if you're feeling nervous on the day.

And thinking about your structure, at what stage do you think the very climax of your speech should come?

At the very end?

No, surprisingly it's not at the very end. All great speeches - and great works of music, literature and the cinema all have their climatic moment around 90% on their timeline. This allows time for the audience to gently come down from the excitement and briefly reflect on the music, the story or the speech.

A speaker who finishes on a massive high risks looking a touch 'manic' or 'messianic'.

So for 'epic' speeches, it's far better to build up the audience's emotion, climaxing around 90% on your timeline, by which time the audience is hopefully cheering wildly, allowing you to pull back and appear calm and in control, amid the hysteria of the crowd.

But even though most of us don't have to give epic speeches, we should still aim to peak around 90% on our timeline and end with a gentle thought or amusing line. This way we can make even the toughest sales pitch look effortless.

And finally ...

The American wit Dorothy Parker said, 'The two most beautiful words in the English language are 'Cheque enclosed'.

But I can assure you that the two most beautiful words an audience want to hear are 'And finally ...'

There are few things more annoying to an audience than suggesting that you're about to finish and then you don't.

Only say the word 'Finally' once.

Finally should mean *finally*.

EXERCISE 1

Use a Mind Map to write a speech

Try constructing a talk about one of your favourite holidays using a Mind Map. It could be a holiday you had as a child or more recently.

In the centre circle write your holiday location.

And in a series of circles coming from that write in the things that made it so special. Who you went with. What you did. Would you go back there? Was it long enough? Would you recommend it?

You get the idea.

The point of Mind Maps is that we aren't trying to write a speech in long hand or type it out fully on our computer. We're trying to get at the bare bones of the subject, the areas that you might want to cover.

At this stage write everything down. We're brainstorming here, don't over edit, just put it all down. You can easily edit out later.

Using Mind Maps makes structuring a talk really easy.

Hopefully you'll end up with a several logical strands of information and ideas.

We always start delivering the talk from the centre, with our Headline. Then we have to decide which of the various strands we will follow first.

Chose the order of the strands in a logical sequence to keep you and your audience on track.

Try telling this story using your Mind Map as your notes.

Don't be tempted to write it all out, try to speak just using the Mind Map.

See if it becomes easier to speak if you use your own words spontaneously rather than reading out a complete script.

Here is an example of what a Mind Map might look like:

EXERCISE 2

The five heartbeats

Now try to adapt your opening sentence from the last exercise into five heartbeats - iambic pentameter.

Using our Mind Map holiday example, the initial sentence in iambic pentameter, might become:

'In Rome I fell in love and changed my life.'

Try saying this out loud hitting the five heartbeat rhythms.

It might not always be appropriate, or even necessary, to use iambic pentameter but it's a good fun exercise and sometimes the results are worth it.

EXERCISE 3

The 50 Word Story

The writer James Joyce said that one of his greatest regrets in life was that he hadn't written *Ulysses* in 50 words. In fact, it ended up at about 265,000 words, and he used an impressive lexicon of over 30,000 different words.

Don't worry, I'm not going to ask you to condense *Ulysses* into 50 words.

I'd like you to write your holiday story in exactly 50 words. Not 48 or 49, not 51 or 52, but exactly 50 words. It's a really good exercise and it sharpens your thoughts. There is no space for waffle in 50 words. Every word must count.

When you've written your 50 words, read them out loud.

It's extraordinary how much sharper our writing becomes when we have chosen each and every word carefully.

EXERCISE 4

The Fairy Tale Template

Think of a subject for a talk or a presentation and then try slotting it into the Fairy Tale template:

1. Once upon a time there was a ...
2. They used to do this ...
3. Then one day something changed ...
4. So they ...
5. And as a result they ...

See if this either helps or changes how the speech might work.

EXERCISE 5

Try different openings

Using your speech idea from the last exercise, try out some different openings with the Headline Method.

Write down five different openings that could start your talk with:

The Hook

The Tease

The Quiz

The Shock

The Three Way Opening

Now read them each out loud.

How did they sound and feel?

Does one work better than another in this particular situation?

EXERCISE 6

Think about your audience

Before you start to structure a talk or a presentation, ask yourself these ten questions:

1 What is my relationship with the audience?

2 How much do they know about me?

3 Are they my peers, superiors, subordinates?

4 What do they think of me? How much credibility do I have with them? (Age, gender, race, experience, etc.)

5 What is my goal - to inform, sell, persuade, motivate, anger, harmonise, neutralize, create controversy?

6 What do they want from me?

7 What do I want from them?

8 What other factors may influence how they see me?

9 Why should they care about what I have to say?

10 What's in it for them?

7

Your Delivery

OK, your big day has arrived and it's time to deliver your talk.

How should you deliver it to maximum effect? Do you bounce on stage like a professional comedian? Or enter with the gravitas of a world leader?

The answer depends totally on you, your own particular style, your message, the occasion, the audience, the venue and the time of day.

We should remember that we have been given a great responsibility when we give a speech. We are asking an audience to give up their valuable time to sit and listen to us. It is our duty to respect the audience's commitment in being there and to prepare and deliver our talk to the best of our ability.

There are many different ways and styles to give our talk but all communication, whether it actually involves giving a speech or not, requires three things: Energy, Clarity and Humanity.

Energy, in that we all need slightly more energy than we think we do need. We're not necessarily looking for the high energy of a TV game show host - although sometimes that might be appropriate, of course - but try to lift the energy of the room an extra 10% as you enter. Feel like you're lighting the up the room. Energy is infectious and it looks like you want to be there.

Clarity, that's clarity of thought, clarity of message, clarity of delivery. So that the listener will understand and remember what you've said.

And lastly, humanity. In a world where electronic communication has almost entirely taken over, the fact that you are one human being who has bothered to turn up and reach out to another human being gives you an immediate head start. People respond to people. We all want to feel engaged and valued. Humanity is vital.

If you think of all the great speakers you've ever seen, either live or on television, they will have had these three essential qualities, energy, clarity and humanity.

These are qualities we all have inside us - we're born with them. But as we grow up we are often told to hide our emotions; this happens to children as young as playground age, and by doing this we cut off one of the most powerful communication tools we have.

If we can feel comfortable in showing our humanity and our passion, we too can become powerful, charismatic speakers.

To learn or not to learn?

Should we learn the whole speech? Should we use notes, cards or bullet points? Or should we have it all written out in its entirety and read from the script?

Of course, it depends on your personal preference, the situation and how much preparation time you have had.

There are advantages and disadvantages to all of these options.

Reading the entire speech can work well if you have no preparation time. Many clients say they often have to give speeches that are written for them by their team. Hopefully their writers are used to their rhythms, so that even when they're sight reading it, they can make it sound as if are saying their own words.

But there are three potential problems with reading the whole speech from a script. The first is that you are less able to keep eye contact with the audience. Secondly, you are less able to walk about and can become tied to your lectern. And lastly, written sentences tend to be longer and more complicated than spoken ones.

I mentioned in Chapter 6 that only the truly great minds of playwrights and intellectuals can think spontaneously in sub-clauses, so unless you are very clever, reading a written speech can easily sound stilted.

One of my heroes, Charles Dickens, could write marathon sentences of great clarity, and he read his books out loud - but it is a rare gift. You can help yourself by using shorter, more colloquial sentences whenever possible.

On BBC Radio 4 in the mornings, there is often a *Thought for the Day* given by an eminent religious or community leader. The speakers generally read from a complete transcript of their speech as they have been given strict timings. They often have a quick chat with the host of the show before speaking. So, first, we hear them speak in their 'own voice' to the host, then we hear their voice change as they start to read from their script.

We know immediately that they have started to 'read' by this marked change in their voice and somehow it sounds false.

One of the best talks I heard recently was from the screen writer Richard Curtis (*Four Weddings and a Funeral/Notting Hill*). He read the whole speech and it worked perfectly. But then he is a particularly fine and funny writer. I remember thinking that he must have spent a good deal of time and thought constructing it. It showed a huge respect for the audience that he was prepared to put in the time to write it so carefully.

Learning the whole speech is only an option if you have enough time to learn it, it's not too long and you are a good learner. It's wonderful if you are able to learn it. It can sound spontaneous and hopefully the audience will believe that you mean what you say. A downside is that with the pressure of the big day you might forget what you were going to say - although this can easily be covered up by having a copy of the speech to hand, just in case.

There is a slight danger that it might sound like you have learned it by rote unless you have had some experience of speaking, which could sound artificial. But generally, I would say if you feel up to learning it, give it a go. It's very impressive when speakers have no notes - and audiences love it.

Bullet points or notes on cards can work well. They can fit easily into your jacket pocket or your handbag and, if made of card, and they tend not to shake as much as paper does should you ever get a little nervous.

You can either write out your notes in traditional bullet point style, as here:

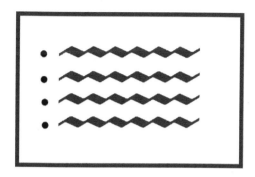

Or in Mind Map form, as here:

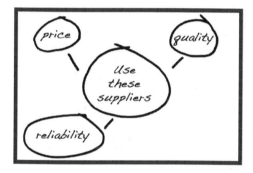

I have seen speakers have their notes on an iPad, either saved as a continuous document or as a series of pdf pages. The first requires continuous scrolling and the second repetitive swiping. Both can be distracting to an audience.

If you place cards on a lectern, you might be better off writing your notes on the top half of an A4 sheet. This will keep your eye line higher so you lose less contact with the audience.

Choose whichever method works best for you. And remember you can use different colours too. So if you went for bullet points, you could write most of the words in black but write the third point in red. This not only makes it stand out but your eye will know if you are above or below the red line which will stop you losing your place as you look up to the audience.

If you can't use colour, you could use an arrow to give yourself an anchor mark on the card, as here:

And remember, if you do use notes or cards, don't pretend that you aren't using them by holding them down by your side and furtively sneaking an occasional look.

It's a mark of respect to your audience that you have taken the time to prepare your talk, so rather than being embarrassed about having notes, hold them up proudly.

Check out the space

I remember the first time I walked out on to the stage at the London Palladium for a dress rehearsal. It's a big theatre with around 2,400 seats. I had been an actor for over twenty years at that point but the London Palladium was a world-famous theatre and it had a huge Wow factor - it almost took my breath away.

We talk about great actors and speakers who *own the stage*. What does it mean? Well, that they feel relaxed there. And they look as relaxed as they feel. They had probably checked out the space beforehand. They weren't surprised by how big the auditorium felt when they first walked on stage.

All speakers should check out the room first.

Think about where to position yourself, making sure that you aren't partially hidden. It's a basic rule that if you can't see some of the faces of the audience, then they can't see yours.

Walk around the stage, see how long it takes to walk from the side to the podium. If there's no obvious place to speak from, then decide where you will stand. Make all those decisions before you get up there for real.

Say a few sentences out loud from the stage. Work out how much volume you need. When using a microphone, ask the sound department if you can have a quick sound check. Let the microphone do the work, don't be tempted to look at the back row, 50 meters away, and try to reach there with you own voice.

The two second pause

Let me tell you a quick story. My stepson's Headmaster retired and the Head of History was appointed as the new Headmaster.

He gave a welcome speech to all the parents and asked me afterwards how I thought it had gone. I told him that it had been pretty good but that he had come across more like a Head of History and less like a Headmaster.

He asked me what he could have done differently. 'Just one thing,' I said. 'Wait for two seconds before you speak.'

This two second pause does several things. Firstly, it gives you time to look at the audience and check that they are ready to listen. There's no point speaking if they're all chattering to their friends or texting on their mobiles.

Secondly, it pulls their focus to you, so that they will hear your first well-chosen words. It would be a shame if all that hard preparation were wasted because they weren't listening.

And lastly, it says that you are comfortable just being there. If you start too quickly it gives the impression that you want to get it over with and get off the stage as soon as you can.

A common question asked by newly qualified teachers is, 'How do I not lose my voice when I'm trying to be heard over twenty shrieking teenagers?'

The answer, of course, is don't try to be louder than twenty shrieking teenagers in the first place. You can't, so don't try. What you can do is wait until they stop. This is a longer version of the two second pause. Eventually they will stop and then, very calmly, you can start the lesson.

Authority figures who shout out of frustration lose both their authority and their voice. Shouting, 'Quiet!' doesn't do it. Waiting till the audience is ready says a lot about you. The audience's instant judgement of you will be 'calm authority.' And that's what we're after.

I don't like housekeeping notices at the start of a talk. I think they set the wrong tone. I was at a wedding recently where the priest said, 'Before we start, can I say that there should be no photography during the service and please do not throw confetti in the churchyard as it is a nightmare to clean up afterwards. Now can we all start by singing the opening hymn.'

But the loving atmosphere of the wedding had already evaporated.

If housekeeping notices have to be given, then they could be better done by the host rather than the speaker, or they could be printed in the literature or handouts.

We want to come across as having credibility and rapport, we don't want to come across as a policeman.

So walk onto the platform, look at the audience and wait two seconds before you speak, centre yourself, making sure your feet are even weight, tighten your buttocks or your thighs, breathe into your stomach, and off you go ...

Stay present

One of the best speakers I've ever heard was Oliver McTernan, a former Catholic priest and now an inter-faith leader. He always spoke without notes and with great authenticity.

As he left the parish after twenty years he said to his congregation, 'If you remember nothing that I have said over the last twenty years, try to remember this. Be present in all you do. Just be present.'

We should always try to be 'present' when we give a talk.

When we go to the theatre, we want to feel that it's the first time that this story has ever been told. Even if we have seen the play before we want to be surprised at the twists and turns of the story. Actors in a long run of a play have the problem of keeping it fresh night after night. I once played in *The King and I* at the London Palladium. Eight shows a week for a year. Each and every one of those 415 nights (we didn't play on Christmas Day) was the first time that that particular audience had seen that show. It had to be special for them. It forced us to be present.

An actor playing Hamlet saying the famous lines, 'To be or not to be? That is the question', has to imagine that it's the first time he has ever said those words. He can't say, 'To be or not to be? That is the question. In fact, it's the same question I asked myself at the matinée this afternoon.' If we stay present, so will the audience.

I am a huge tennis fan and feel really sorry for players faced with rain delays. Just when their minds and bodies are in full flow, the rain comes along and interrupts their flow. What is going through their minds as they limber up or sit in the dressing room waiting? They must stay present and focussed. They are great examples of staying present at a high professional level.

Live TV and radio presenters often have an odd speech pattern when they are thinking about the next thing they are going to say. They slow down the last few words of a sentence and seem to be saying them automatically while their brain is off thinking about the next sentence.

They can sound rather like the contestants on *Just A Minute*, the brilliant BBC Radio panel game, who are not allowed any hesitation, deviation or repetition. In the show it's used to comic advantage but stretching out a sentence whilst thinking about the next one usually loses connection with an audience.

If we are thinking about the next thing we are going to say, we tend to lose track and make a mistake. I often see speakers fluff or tumble over a line just before they say a joke. What has probably happened is that whilst they've been speaking, their mind has leapt ahead and they have started worrying about delivering the upcoming joke. As a result they stumble on both the current sentence and the joke.

Try to remember that we are often much better than we think we are - and that if we focus on the sentence we are in, then we should be fine.

Pace

When reading a book on our own, we generally read between 250 and 300 words a minute.

Copy typists can type over 150 words a minute, while two-finger typists (like me) key in at about 40 words a minute. And when using our best handwriting, we write at about 35 words a minute.

People tend to dictate to computers at about 100 words a minute.

Audience's attention spans have shortened over time. The average political sound bite has changed in length, from 43 seconds in 1968 to around 9 seconds today.

Ideally, as we talk, we will vary our pace to keep the audience alert. But what is the ideal speed when giving a talk or a presentation?

The formula used in radio production is around three words a second, which is a comfortable and understandable pace for most people. It might slow down to two words a second if they are dealing with longer or more complicated words.

When Steve Jobs launched a new Apple product, he typically spoke at 158 words a minute. But those were well chosen words in perfectly constructed sentences, with lots of practice.

150 words is just under half an A4 page of double spaced type at 12 font. So a full page of A4 should take you around 2 minutes to deliver.

As an experiment, try saying this sentence out loud:

'Pizza tastes good with pepperoni and sausage.'

Now time yourself as you read those seven words again.

The fastest I can say it in clearly is just under two seconds, and in just under three seconds for a more comfortable read.

That would work out at 210 or 140 words a minute respectively. And once I've added in pauses for emphasis it would drop down to 180 or 120 words a minute - the formula used in radio production.

But, of course, it will always depend on the type of talk we are giving, the audience and the speaker's ability to articulate clearly.

I think it's usually best to aim for around 150 words a minute when presenting or giving a talk.

The power of the pause

'The music is in the silence between the notes.'
(Claude Debussy)

If we want our audience to hear our well-chosen words and thoughts, then they need space around them. And they need time to process the information we give them.

The 1930's pottery designer Susie Cooper felt that the space around a pattern was as important as the pattern itself. If a plate was covered in little blue stars with no space around them at all, then it would basically be a blue plate. But the more space there is around a few well-chosen little blue stars, the more we really notice them.

I often hear speakers say, 'I want you to think about that.' But then they carry straight on without having given us any time to actually think about it.

Pausing is also useful as it can interrupt the brain patterns of the audience. How often have we heard speakers who have got into a repetitive phrasing? This can send us to sleep very easily. Especially if the end of their sentences have a repetitive dying fall. However, if we pause on a particular word or at the end of a thought, we can break this pattern.

Picking out key words

Get into the habit of picking out key words as you speak. Emphasising the right word can often change the meaning of the sentence. It also stops every word having the same value, which helps against it sounding monotonous.

Try reading this sentence out loud:

'I know you like your brand-new suit.'

This sentence has eight different meanings depending on how you stress or emphasize the words.

Now try putting the stress on the underlined word:

'I know you like your brand-new suit.'
(I know but other people might not)

'I know you like your brand-new suit.'
(I know because you've told me)

'I know you like your brand-new suit.'
(You might like it but many people might not)

'I know you like your brand-new suit.'
(But perhaps it is not appropriate to wear it today)

'I know you like your brand-new suit.'
(But you don't like mine)

'I know you like your brand-new suit.'
(But your old one might have been more appropriate)

'I know you like your brand-new suit.'
(But that tie is a disaster)

Emphasizing key words with a pause

Try saying this sentence out loud,

'Unless we can sort this out by December, we are going to have huge problems next year.'

What is the most important word in that sentence? Many people would suggest that it is *problems*. But that doesn't really help us understand the issue.

I think what we want them to realise is that if we sort this out by *December*, then all might be OK.

So try saying the sentence out loud, emphasizing *December*.

'Unless we can sort this out by <u>December</u>, we are going to have huge problems next year.'

Now try saying it again, but add the words *ONE TWO* into the sentence, as here:

'Unless we can sort this out by ONE TWO, <u>December</u>, ONE TWO, we are going to have huge problems next year.'

Now say it again but counting the *'ONE TWO's* in your head before and after the word.

This will effectively pick out that word. The audience will clearly hear that word and realise that if they sort this out by *December* all might be well.

'Unless we can sort this out by ... <u>December</u>, ... we are going to have huge problems next year.'

By picking out the key word and pointing the audience to that word, we are giving them time to really hear it and to process the information. They are less likely to drift away into their own thoughts and hopefully will stay glued to your message.

We are all familiar with the success of Barack Obama's memorable phrase, *'Yes, we can'*. Interestingly, the official transcript of his speech at the New Hampshire primary punctuates the famous sentence like this: *'Yes. We. Can.'*

What to wear

You must feel comfortable in what you are wearing. You don't want to feel restricted or tight.

Choose clothes that make you feel good.

But remember that the audience will be watching you for quite a while. After a minute or two, assuming you are appropriately dressed, the audience will probably stop looking at your outfit; however, eccentric clothing or odd socks will probably get noticed.

As a general rule, I usually advise dressing slightly better than your audience. We should always show respect to our audience.

Technology

Technology is a mixed blessing. When it works it can add tremendous value and interest. Clear charts and powerful images. When it doesn't work it's a nightmare.

So, if you are going to use slides, always back up them up on an external hard drive or on a CD in case your computer goes down. And if you bring them on a USB stick, bring them on a spare one too in case that goes down.

It's also a good idea to print out your presentation on paper as a back up, in case the entire system goes down.

Bring every conceivable lead you have that might be useful. Computer and AV equipment is not always compatible.

I once gave a talk at one of the most famous film and broadcasting companies in the world. I called the AV department the day before to check on what equipment I should bring along. They said, 'Relax, this is our industry. We know what we're doing.'

Guess what?

Their equipment didn't work of the day of the talk. Since then I never take any chances. In fact, I rarely use slides at all.

PowerPoint

OK, so we have to talk about PowerPoint - surely the most ubiquitous communication tool around.

Most people can't even say the words without apologising or sneering. And yet we see it being used all the time. Apple's Keynote may be slightly easier to use but is essentially the same tool. And even the whizzy Prezi, with its zooming white board, is a way of putting your talk up on a screen.

Four reasons to have a slide

Before we start constructing a slide deck let's look at the four reasons for having slides in a PowerPoint deck.

1. To state your argument.

2. To develop your argument.

3. To add new information to the argument.

4. To start a new area/section to your presentation.

If we start constructing from this standpoint, our deck should tell a story and take our audience on a logical journey.

Here are ten thoughts on the use of PowerPoint:

1. What to put on a slide

I'm sure you're aware of the basic rules when composing your slides, so I won't spend too much time on that here. Ideally, use big font, with no more than five bullet points on a slide and no more than five words per bullet - known as the 5 x 5 Rule.

We should always try to make it easy for the audience to read the words. Too small a font and they get frustrated because it's too difficult to read. Too many words and they start reading ahead instead of listening to you.

The same goes for indices on graphs. I often struggle to know what the A and B axis refer to. If you have to have small indices, you can help the audience by telling them what they mean: 'This graph shows our performance over the last five years.'

2. Should the audience look at me or at the screen?

When presenting a deck, there is always a big dilemma for an audience. Should they look at the speaker or should they look at the screen?

This is where we, as speakers, have to be clever. We must tell the audience when to look at us and when to look at the screen. At all times. If we let their eyes roam freely we have lost them.

If you want them to look at you, take a small step away from the screen and they will look at you. This could even be as subtle as shifting your weight away from the screen.

And when you want them to look back and read something, glance or shift your weight back towards the screen and that's exactly where they will look.

Always tell them where to look.

3. Don't speak to the slide

Try to avoid the temptation to talk to the screen.

The screen seems to suck a speaker in, almost like a safety blanket. If we're not quite sure about how to phrase the next sentence we will often look to the screen for inspiration.

Try to fight this urge.

Instead, look at the audience for inspiration. Two seconds of thinking time looking at the audience is better than two seconds of thinking time looking at the screen. The audience doesn't want to see the back of your head.

Be careful not to favour one side of the audience. Sometimes we get so wrapped up in what we were saying that we don't realize we're ignoring half the audience.

Speakers often find themselves speaking more to one side of a room than the other. This could be because the computer or the screen is set to one side, or because we simply feel more comfortable looking one way rather than the other. In the same way that when we're reversing in a car, it is often easier to turn to one side than the other.

So if necessary, vary where you stand. Go for a wander every now and then, move from one side of the screen to the other.

4. Announce the slide before you click the button

This is one of the simplest ways to look really good when using PowerPoint.

If you announce the slide before you click the button it looks like you have done your homework, that you know what's coming next and that you're in control of the Powerpoint slides, rather than either being a slave to them or using them as your script.

Here's an example:

(THE OPENING SLIDE IS SHOWING ON SCREEN)

'Have you ever wanted X? Well, today, I'm going to tell you how you can get X. But let's first have a look at why so many of us feel that we can't have X.'

(CLICK THE BUTTON FOR THE NEXT SLIDE)

'As you can see, there are five main reasons.'

5. Stop them reading ahead

The easiest way to stop an audience reading ahead is to tell them where to look on the slide

As soon as you have clicked the slide, the audience is suddenly presented with new information. Their eyes will be darting around to decide where to look. Be really clear, so they know which line or part of the slide you're talking about.

So, let's continue with our PowerPoint example:

'As you can see, there are five main reasons. Let's take a look at them one by one. Firstly, on the top line, TOO EXPENSIVE. Yes, many people think that X will be too expensive. It's a lovely product and I can see why they might well think that. Next, on the second line, BELIEF. They never had the belief that they could ever actually own one.'

You must tell them immediately which line you are on. If you leave it even a second their eyes will be off and they'll be reading ahead.

So as soon as the slide appears tell them physically where to look. Make it easy for them by using different colours.

'You can see from the first line in <u>green</u> that ...' or

'This graph shows the last ten years. Our performance, on the top line, is in <u>red</u>. The rest of the market is below, in <u>blue</u>.'

You get the idea. The audience are not left guessing what the lines on the graph refer to. They're not guessing what the indices are. They don't even have to try to read them because you have told them. You have made it easy for them. And if you make it easy for them, they will listen to you, rather than blanking you out while they try to work it out for themselves.

The same applies if you are presenting a printed slide deck at a seated meeting. You still have to direct the audience where to look to stop them reading ahead. But they have control over the deck and can easily turn over and start to read other pages rather than concentrating on the one you are talking about.

A simple technique, right at the start, is to put your hand firmly on top of the closed deck in front of you. This gives a clear, but subliminal, signal to the audience not to turn their pages over just yet.

So, with your hand firmly on the top of your printed slide deck, 'As you have had this in advance, I am not going to go through every page today. I think it would be more helpful if I picked out the parts that I think are most relevant for you. So if we can all turn to page three. As you can see on the <u>red</u> chart, in the middle of the page ...'

You can keep them looking at the page you are on by directing them exactly where to look.

6. Say the exact words that appear on the slide

Imagine the top line of a slide says: TOO EXPENSIVE.

Instead of saying the exact words that appear on the screen, many speakers will say something like 'A lot of people think they can't afford it.'

This is a very common mistake. It might have the same meaning but the audience is now searching for the words CAN'T AFFORD IT. It's distracting for them because those words aren't there.

If audiences are confused they will stop listening. Your job is to make it really, really easy for them to follow your message.

This would be better:

'TOO EXPENSIVE. Yes, many people think that X might be too expensive.'

7. Know the reason why every slide is there

I was once coaching a sales team in the north of England where the company had a generic PowerPoint slide deck that all potential customers were shown. The third slide was titled, THE HISTORY OF OUR COMPANY.

It had twenty-five lines on in it. Yes, twenty-five. At the top of the screen, on the left hand side, was the date 1903. This was when the company was founded. The dates continued for another twenty-four lines until it reached 2013. Beside each date was an important milestone for the company. For example, 1918, opened an office in Manchester. 1927, opened a branch in Liverpool. 1983, outsourced its Account Department, etc. You're probably bored already, and I've only picked out three lines.

I finally stopped one salesman and said. 'I'm a potential customer. I don't care whether your office is in Liverpool or not. I just want to hear about your product.' He said that he had to go through this slide because his boss told him he had too.

I asked the 200 strong team why that slide was there at all. One of them said, 'To establish that the company has been going a long time and has a good track record.'

I asked him to do the slide again, knowing that. So then he said, 'This slide shows the history of our company. As you can see we've been going over a hundred years, we know what we're doing. Relax, you can trust us.'

Now the slide has done its job. The only purpose of that slide was to establish 'trust'. If he had gone through the whole slide and not told us how to 'feel', it would have been a missed opportunity and merely bored the audience to distraction.

Always tell the audience how to feel about a slide.

Every slide should be there for a purpose. It should advance your argument, reassure or challenge the audience in some way, or introduce a new idea.

If we remember that, then we will never just 'go through' the slides.

8. A screen show or a printed handout?

There is a difference between a printed deck that you hand out to your audience in a seated meeting and a deck to be shown on a screen. We can read small fonts and indices on a printed sheet but will struggle to read them on the screen.

Clients often tell me they have a problem because they have to send out the slide deck in advance. Then they present the same deck on a screen at the actual meeting.

But a written deck and a screen deck are not and should not be the same.

If you have to send out a written deck in advance, make a copy of the written slide deck on your computer and then edit that copy. Take out most of the words, keeping only the essential core of your message. Then, as you speak, interpret and explain the meaning of the slides for your audience. If they have been given the slides in advance, your talk isn't exactly going to be a surprise.

What will keep their interest is your interpretation of the information. Tell them why it's interesting, new, worrying, or exciting.

9. Never just give information

If you said flatly, 'The sales figures for last quarter were one million dollars', the audience won't necessarily know if that's good news or bad. Or indeed how good or bad.

Don't leave their interpretation to chance. Tell them how you feel about it.

'There's some great news here... (CLICK then smile) ... the sales figures for last quarter were one million dollars!'

If you think it's good, then tell them. They can agree or disagree with you, but always tell them how you feel.

10. Transitions

A good technique which works well is to ask a question at the end of a slide, which is then answered by the next slide:

For example, 'But how can we make this happen? (CLICK TO NEXT SLIDE) There are three main ways. And here they are.'

This keeps the talk constantly moving forward, each slide linking to the next one, towards the final conclusion.

Be careful of wacky and whizzy transitions - they can be distracting and repetitive. Rather than listen to the speaker, we can sit there waiting to see which transition the speaker will use next.

My final thought on PowerPoint

We have got so used to using PowerPoint as a tool that we often forget to ask ourselves if a slide deck is the best way to tell our story or if we really need it for this particular talk.

Perhaps there is a section where we needn't use slides at all. Could we, instead, use our own words and go freestyle for a bit? It might break up the talk and inject some new energy in the middle.

Imagine if Churchill had given his '*We will fight them on the beaches*' speech using PowerPoint. Or if Abraham Lincoln had given his *Gettysburg Address* using Powerpoint.

I suspect both speeches would have lost much of their power. And surely that's the point.

Nerves on the day

Many speakers tell me they would rather keep to themselves for the last few minutes before making a speech or giving a presentation to gather their thoughts. I can see their logic but there are several missed opportunities here.

Firstly, speaking to someone immediately before you go on distracts you from any nerves you might have. In his book, *The Inner Game of Tennis*, W. Timothy Gallwey explains that most of us play tennis much better and more freely when we are warming up, than we do in a match, where we tend to tense up.

What Gallwey says is that we should 'distract' ourselves just before we hit the ball, so we slip back into our relaxed pre-match state.

When playing tennis in a match, he suggests trying to focus on reading the writing on the ball as it comes towards you, Penn, Slazenger, Dunlop or whatever. I tried it and it really works.

I've tried this in a speech scenario too. If you distract yourself just before you are about to speak you temporarily take the focus off your nerves.

So have a quick word with someone. Notice a stain on the carpet or a bulb missing in the ceiling lights. Anything that distracts you for a brief second.

Secondly, if you haven't spoken for a few minutes it will be a shock when you open your mouth on stage. You won't have heard your voice for a bit and have no idea if it's working properly, if you have a 'frog' in your throat or how loud you are.

So it's a good idea to speak to someone immediately before you walk onto the stage or podium. A quick 'Are we ready to go?' to the organizer is enough - just to hear how your voice is sounding.

Thirdly, chatting with a member of the audience before you start is a great way to establish rapport and make new friends. It helps having a few friendly faces in the audience beaming back at you when you first start.

And if you have mingled with the audience before you speak, you can always say, 'I was talking about this to Bob from Accounts a few moments ago ...' Again, you are establishing rapport - the *ethos* that Aristotle talks about.

And lastly, if you chat to your audience before you start you can gauge their mood. It's always good to know how they might be feeling. Are they looking forward to your talk or are they worried about what you might have to say? As I said earlier, always acknowledge the elephant in the room.

As you start you want to be enthusiastic - enthusiasm is infectious. But we don't want our high levels of adrenalin to tip our enthusiasm into manic or pushy. Calm, confident enthusiasm is what we're after here.

But before your big moment arrives, and you are introduced, remember the audience will judge you in the *blink* of an eye. So it's vital to get the first ten seconds right.

Let's go over our pre-talk warm up exercises.

Warm up Exercises

Let's get warmed up, focused and centred with these four, short warm up exercises.

1. From a standing position, bend forward - as if trying to touch your toes. Stretch the back of the knees gently three times. You are not, in fact, trying to touch your toes but getting rid of any tension in the legs.

As you straighten up, you will feel that you stand taller. You will also have sent some blood back into your brain - always good before giving a talk.

2. Roll your shoulders three times, forward and backwards. This loosens any tension in the upper chest and neck.

3. Wake the face up by chewing an imaginary piece of toffee. Make really silly faces. Wide, tight, left and right.

4. Stick your tongue out as far as you can and say the whole of *Humpty Dumpty*. As we have discovered, this opens the back of the throat and brings the voice forward, making it sound more centred and open.

These four exercises should have got rid of any pre-talk jitters - and they take under a minute.

If you feel a sense of rising panic, remember that it is simply your body responding with its characteristic fight or flight response. It's better to have a little panic now rather than have a full blown attack when you get started. Get it out of the way now, so you can enjoy the ride.

If you find yourself feeling a bit nervous, try the gentle breathing exercise from page 71. Breathe in and out through your nose for a count of three. Do this three times. You will lower your heart rate and feel calmer.

Before you Start

Your big moment has finally arrived.

Here's a 10 point pre-talk check list for you to go through just before you start:

1. Eating and drinking: A little food is good half an hour before you speak but try to avoid dairy products. Cheese or yoghurt will line your throat and muffle your voice. Coffee will dry out your throat. I would avoid the temptation to drink alcohol before you speak. Water is best.

2. Go to the bathroom (believe me, you do not want a full bladder when presenting).

3. Check yourself in the mirror (unruly hair, spinach in the teeth, unzipped flies, shirts not tucked in, etc.).

4. Put a tissue in your pocket (sneezing in public without a tissue does not look good).

5. Turn off your phone - or if you are expecting an urgent call give it to a friend to answer for you.

6. Check you have your notes in your pocket (if you are using them).

7. Know the first sentence you'll say.

8. Do your four warm up exercises.

9. Breathe.

10. Smile.

And away you go ...

At the end

You want to end well. Your audience wants you to end well.

So once you have said your final sentence, you still have one more thing to say. The audience have to know that it really is the end of your speech and not merely a long pause for dramatic effect.

The best way I have found to end a talk is to say, *'Thank you very much.'*

Then the audience is in no doubt that you have completely finished.

I have also discovered that saying *'Thank you'* will not get the same level of applause as saying *'Thank you very much.'*

The rhythm works better. Try it for yourself.

And having said *'Thank you very much'* - stop talking. It is tempting to keep on talking but it will undermine your clean ending.

After waiting two seconds for your applause to start, you can then move back to your seat.

If you move too early, it looks as if you are desperate to get the whole thing over with as quickly as possible and can't wait for the safety of your own seat.

So after finishing your talk, say *'Thank you very much'*, wait two seconds for the applause to start, then move back to your seat - feeling very proud of yourself.

Question and Answer Sessions

Actors can get to the end of a performance and feel elated but speakers often get to the end of a speech and find themselves panicking because of the dreaded Question and Answer session immediately following.

Clients often tell me that this is the most nerve-wracking part of their talk.

The first thing to do with questions is to listen.

By that I mean really listen to the question - right to the end. Resist the temptation to come in too quickly with your answer.

Listening carefully, means that you:

1. answer the right question.
2. show respect to the questioner by valuing their question
3. have enough thinking time to answer it well.

In Aboriginal culture it is expected that you take a long time to answer a question; they are comfortable with silence during their conversation. But in many other cultures people want to jump in and answer quickly. Resist that temptation in Question and Answer time. Listen carefully.

What if no-one asks a question?

People are often nervous to ask a question from the floor, so try encouraging them by saying, 'Every question's a great question.' Then when someone does ask a question, you can say, 'That's a great question.' (And you'll probably get a nice laugh.)

And if no-one puts their hand up, you could say, 'I was talking to someone earlier who asked me ...' (Even if they hadn't.)

What if you are not sure how to answer the question?

Try repeating the question, as if you're really thinking about how to answer it. 'Why do I believe X? (TAKE TIME TO THINK) Because of these reasons ...'

Or repeat the question to help the audience, 'I don't know if you could hear that at the back, but the question was ...'

Or: 'I don't have those figures to hand today, but if you let me have your email address at the end, I'll gladly send them over to you.'

What if someone is not really asking a question but merely stating their point?

If you don't want to get drawn down a blind alley with this one simply say, 'Thank you, that's an interesting point of view. Next question.'

What if they are opposed to your views and pretend to offer you two answers, both of which make you look bad?

As here: 'Surely you're really only doing this either to save the company money or to save the shareholders money?'
Try not to get drawn in to this one. Instead restate your case. 'I think the main issue here is that we are, in fact, creating jobs ...'

What if a questioner goes on too long and won't shut up?

Try asking for their name. 'I'm sorry, I didn't catch your name?' (They tell you it's David) 'Thank you, David. I appreciate your thoughts, but I'd like to fit in a few more questions if I can.' Often saying their name clearly will help you control the situation.

What if someone is being aggressive?

Never copy their tone of voice. Speak slowly and gently, and restate their question - this will give you time to change the energy of their tone.

Here are some examples that can 'bridge' from their aggressive tone to your reasonable reply:

'I think what you're really asking is …'

'A better question might be …'

'Let me answer you in this way …'

'I prefer to spend my time with you today discussing what is really important - which is …'

'What's important to remember is …'

Or you could say what Jack Benny said after Fred Allen insulted him, 'You wouldn't say that if my writers were here.'

Or try this great put down, 'I'd like to agree with you - but it I did, we'd both be wrong.'

I once heard a wonderfully funny reply to an aggressive question:

'I'm not really sure how to answer that, but I assure you I'm coming into this with an open kimono.'

I don't know what the speaker actually meant but it deflected a difficult question and he got a huge laugh.

EXERCISE 1

Pace

Let's see what pace of delivery works best for you.

Turn to pages 176-177 and find the section on 'Pace'.

This has a total of 350 words.

Time yourself as you speak this section out loud.

If you spoke for two minutes you would have been speaking at 175 words a minute.

Two and a half minutes would have been at 140 words a minute.

Three minutes would have been at 116 words a minute.

Now try this exercise again and record yourself when speaking. Just record your voice, don't be tempted to use video. It will be easier to listen to your pace if you are not distracted visually.

As you listen back, think about your audience.

Were you speaking too fast?

Or were you speaking at a comfortable rate for them to hear and process your words clearly?

Experiment by trying this exercise several times.

EXERCISE 2

Varying the pace

We want to avoid an even, flat speed of delivery; so using the 'Pace' section from the last exercise let's now try to vary your pace.

Remembering what we learned in the sections on 'Picking out key words' and 'Emphasising key words with a pause' (pages 179-181), I want you now to underline one or two key words in each sentence of the 'Pace' section.

Once you've underlined your chosen words, try reading it out loud and record yourself again.

As you speak, you can either emphasise an underlined word by putting a pause before or after it, by slowing the word down or by varying your volume.

Play the recording back and imagine you are in an audience, listening.

Did this exercise change your overall speed of delivery?

Did it vary your pace?

Did some ways of emphasising these words work better than others?

Was it easier to listen to if you did or didn't emphasise words?

Try this exercise a several different ways.

EXERCISE 3

Build a PowerPoint presentation

Use the 'Pace' section that we've been working on to build a PowerPoint presentation, which should include all the information covered there.

Start by roughly sketching out your slides on paper. I find this is better than going straight to the computer, where we can easily get distracted by trying to make the slides look good with cool fonts and interesting graphics.

So first, let's concentrate on the message.

How should we start to tell our story?

And what do we want the audience to remember at the end?

Once you are happy with your paper slides, start to design your PowerPoint presentation.

The design of PowerPoint slides is a whole subject in itself but I have suggested a couple of helpful books in the Resources section following this chapter.

By way of illustration, I have designed two PowerPoint presentations of the 'Pace' section to demonstrate 'poor' and 'better' PowerPoint practices.

You can view both presentations on my website: www.zone2.co.uk/resources - and then click VIDEO.

You will recognise 'poor' and 'better' practice quite easily.

EXERCISE 4

Video yourself

Now let's have a go at videoing yourself giving a talk or a presentation.

You can either use the 'Pace' section from the last exercise or use a talk that is relevant to you, with or without using PowerPoint.

Once you have decided whether you will learn it or have notes and are ready to go, quickly run through our short warm up exercise routine (p 194) to get you in the mood and press the record button.

Then stand with your weight evenly balanced between both feet and clench your buttocks or your thighs.

Wait two seconds.

And away you go ...

As you play the video back, imagine an audience is watching this talk for the first time. Was your message really clear? Did you make them want to hear it? Were you physically relaxed or were you doing something that might have distracted them from listening to you? Did you look like you wanted to be there?

Clients have often said that when they first watch themselves back on video all they can see is the one physical bit of themselves that they hate; so try to be objective as you watch yourself.

Remember, audiences haven't come to judge you - they have come be entertained.

A final word

We know that many people find the idea of giving a talk or a presentation daunting and, in some cases, even terrifying.

I hope I have shown that speaking in public can be an enjoyable experience and one that you can learn to look forward to.

We don't have to be the best speaker in the world.

We don't have to be the best writer in the world.

We just have to be really clear about what we are saying and what would we like our audience to do or feel as a result.

And if we can learn to say it using our own voice, as *ourselves,* then we will be able to speak with energy, clarity and humanity so that our audience will want to listen.

I wish you the very best of luck on your journey.

Resources

To help with posture, energy and feeling centred

We all want to be able to stand well when we present but more than that, we want to be physically dynamic and relaxed. These disciplines are excellent for performers and speakers:

Pilates: This is particularly good for building up the strength of your core - your centre. Very slow, gentle and powerful. Every movement starts from your centre.

Tai Chi: Again very good for feeling centred. Tai Chi is a set of movements that you can eventually practice at home once you have learned them. As with Pilates, every movement is from your centre. I practiced Tai Chi for a year and loved it.

Yoga: Yoga is great for aligning and toning the body. It is also excellent for breath control. You can join a class initially and then have your own mat at home. I start every day with a short yoga stretch.

The Five Tibetans. These five short exercises are a yoga based routine which takes about 15 minutes to do. You could try reading *The Five Tebetans* by Christopher S. Kilham.

Meditation: There are many forms of meditation. Meditation Mindfulness is very popular - a simple form of stilling the mind. I do this for 15 minutes first thing in the morning before I shower. It is very calming and a lovely way to start the day. It helps me feel centred. There are many books, classes and teaching aids available on Mindfulness Meditation.

To develop your voice

Bone prop

If you feel you would like to work further on your voice and you feel your tongue needs the advance class, you can try using a bone prop.

Try putting two fingers between your top and bottom teeth. Now try to speak. It is hard to articulate but it makes all parts of the mouth work harder.

A bone prop does a similar job. It is a small piece of plastic that fits in between your top and bottom teeth. It holds the mouth open and helps to bring the voice forward and aids articulation training.

I recommend this to clients who really want to develop their voice more fully. It helps with vocal agility. It can slow down your speech rate, increase the space in the oral cavity, encourage resonance, help to bring the sound to the front of the mouth and it builds muscularity in the tongue and the lips.

If you are working with a bone prop, you could try using the articulation exercises from Chapter 4. Be careful not to over-use a bone prop in the early stages to avoid jaw tension. But you will find all the instructions come with it. You can find links to recommended bone props on my website.

Toasts and Introductions

Here are some suggested toasts and introductions that can work well if you are hosting an event:

A toast to a special friend:

'To your good health my old friend,
May you live to be a thousand years
And I be there to count them.'

'May the road rise up to meet you,
May the wind be always at your back.
May the sun shine warm upon your face,
The rains fall soft upon your fields.
And until we meet again,
May God hold you in the palm of His hand.'

A toast to a group of friends:

'May the Lord love us, but not call us too soon.'

'From small beginnings
Unto their undiscovered ends,
Is nothing worth the while of living
Than laughter and the love of friends.'

Introducing a speaker

'I was always told never to have heroes because they will always let you down. But tonight is the exception to the rule. It is my great pleasure to introduce to you this evening ...'

Inviting people to give to a charity

After your talk on behalf of a charity, try ending with this moving, simple prayer that can work as an immediate 'call to action'. I have used this myself and its effects can be profoundly powerful.

'I shall pass through this world but once.
Any good that I can do,
Or any kindness that I can show to any human being,
Let me do it now.
Let me not defer or neglect it,
For I shall not pass this way again.'

(Quaker missionary, Stephen Grellet)

Helpful products

These are two good products I have found to help tired, strained or damaged voices. One is a pastille and one is a spray:

Proctor's Pinelyptus Pastilles are good for singers, public speakers and actors. They are pretty strong and help clear your nose and clear your throat. I like the fact that they are small, so you can hide them in the side of your mouth if suddenly called upon to speak. They are great for clarity of voice and, as they say on the packet, *'They have been used by Lords, Ladies, Principal Public Speakers, Singers and Members of Parliament for over a hundred years'.*

Vocal Eze is a throat spray for tired voices. It is excellent when you have either been talking too much or you've strained your voice. It lasts for ages and a few sprays at the back of the throat can work wonders if you're having problems and you have a big talk coming up. It is glycerine based and soothes over-used, tired, dry and sore throats without chemical and unwanted side effects.

For excessive redness

Green make-up primer. This is applied under make-up and the green neutralises the redness of the skin. Normal skin-coloured foundation can be applied on top. Princess Diana used a green primer on her wedding day. She wasn't prone to redness but with the pressure of the occasion and the heat of the TV lights she was advised to take this precaution.

It is good for people who worry that they might blush excessively when giving a speech. I have used this myself when on TV if I've over-done the sun during the day.

There are many brands available.

For excessive stage fright

Clients have had great results from **homeopathy** and **Bach remedies**. I am not qualified to recommend specific remedies but if nerves are becoming a real problem you might think about seeing a qualified practitioner.

Suggested further reading

Understanding how audiences think

Creative Mischief by Dave Trott

To Sell Is Human by Daniel H. Pink

Persuasion by James Borg

Made To Stick by Chip and Dan Heath

Blink by Malcolm Gladwell

For dealing with performance nerves

The Inner Game Of Tennis by W. Timothy Gallwey

For clever ideas about working with PowerPoint

Slide:Ology by Nancy Duarte

Presentation Zen by Garr Reynolds